recycled home

recycled
home

mark & sally bailey

with photography by debi treloar

LONDON • NEW YORK

Senior designer   Paul Tilby
Senior editor   Clare Double
Location research   Sally Bailey, Emily Westlake
Production manager   Patricia Harrington
Publishing director   Alison Starling

Styling   Mark Bailey

First published in 2007.
This revised edition published in 2013 by
Ryland Peters & Small
20–21 Jockey's Fields, London WC1R 4BW
and
519 Broadway, 5th Floor, New York, NY 10012
www.rylandpeters.com

ISBN: 978 1 84975 356 2

A CIP record from this book is available
from the British Library.

Printed and bound in China.

The original US edition of this book was catalogued as
follows:
Library of Congress Cataloging-in-Publication Data
Bailey, Mark.
  Restoration home / Mark & Sally Bailey ; with
photography by Debi Treloar.
    p. cm.
  Includes index.
  ISBN 978-1-84597-452-7
  1. House furnishings. 2. Recycled products. 3. Building
fittings--Recycling. 4. Found objects (Art) in interior
decoration. I. Bailey, Sally. II. Treloar, Debi. III. Title.
  TX315.B25 2007
  645--dc22
                    2007020729

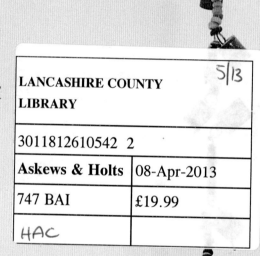

RPS CICO BOOKS
For digital editions visit
rylandpeters.com/apps.php

contents

Rescue, repair, reuse and rethink are the guiding principles of our version of recycling (though we do collect up our newspapers, bottles and jam jars too). We continually track down abandoned, unwanted objects, from old wooden fruit crates to forgotten farm buildings, and give them a new lease of life. When researching this book, we discovered what could be the rumblings of an underground recycling scene – people quietly reviving abandoned things or using unexpected, discarded materials to make furniture. This approach can be applied to your home too.

We recently moved our home and business to a series of interconnecting farm buildings in the Herefordshire countryside. When we first came across Whitecross Farm, it was pretty dilapidated – but it was easy to see the potential in the structure, and we knew something great could grow from it. We wanted to save the buildings from being turned into a barn conversion by developers and restore it as sympathetically as possible. The plan was to avoid turning the farm into something unrecognizable. The past is important and should inform what an old building becomes, so it was important to be true to the bare bones of the well-worn farm, only adding doors and windows where there were previous signs

baileys the philosophy

of them. We also sought out environmentally friendly materials, which often led to old-fashioned

techniques and materials being used – such as lime plaster with yak hair teased into the mixture

(the hair helps it bind together), which is better than modern plaster as it allows the building to

breathe. Sheep's wool was used for much of the insulation. Recycling came into play as well –

about 10,000 old slates were used on the roof. However, for us the recycled look also thrives

on contrasts, so some pretty high-tech materials were employed too – thin layers of space-age

silver foil meant that the roof could be insulated without having to cover up the structure too much.

The things we sell at the farm in the former threshing barn, granary loft, cowshed and

stables are a surprising mix of vintage and new. They come from a variety of sources but all

share the qualities integral to the 'keep it simple, repair and reuse' philosophy. Mark trained

as a furniture maker and has a keen creative eye – ideal for spotting the potential in an unloved

something or other that may turn up on his many trips to closed-down factories or antique

markets across the UK and Europe. Abandoned bobbins from old textile mills appear on the

shelves transformed into egg timers, lamp bases or string holders. We source some products

from small, family-run companies who have been making the same things for generations, such

as beautiful Burleigh pottery, still made in Stoke-on-Trent, or well-made, traditional wooden toys

left unpainted. The organic-as-possible café at Whitecross Farm is also run on the same principles, serving homemade cakes and coffee as well as simple lunches made from local produce. The tables in the café all have mixed-up tops and bottoms as do the stools, which boast contrasting industrial bases with new wooden seats.

Twenty years of rescuing and recycling, and the recent renovation project at Whitecross Farm, have given us the opportunity to establish exactly what our decorating philosophy is: work with what you've got, be true to the structure of your house and the materials it is made from. We think our attitude to home improvement could be summed up by the term 'undecoration' – a word that perfectly describes what we do! You don't necessarily have to add to improve – sometimes it's better to take away. Discover the honesty and history of your house by peeling back its layers of wallpaper and paint. This will give you the chance to see what your house has been through before you came along, and in this way the house itself gives the decorating direction rather than you imposing your will and endless paint charts upon it. Instead you embark upon a voyage of discovery together, and by taking this course you learn to appreciate the creativity there is to be found in imperfection – there's always a surprise in store when you undecorate. It is a much more fulfilling and honest process to work with; you are being true to the basic materials and textures of your home. Utter perfection and sleekly smooth painted walls can rapidly become boring, there is no definition and your eyes skim over the surface all too quickly. Contrasting textures are an important factor in the recycled home and should not be underestimated, as they highlight all the best bits. Stripped wood with crackled and flaky paint, and subtly hued plasterwork sit well with one or two necessarily shiny new additions, such as a stainless-steel worktop added to a rough table to make it more user-friendly and give it an unexpected twist. Mismatched chairs get along just fine: their individuality – the reason you love them in the first place – shines through.

The ability to love surprises and think differently about what might turn up also applies to the things you choose to furnish your home with. Forget preconceived ideas about the purpose of things. This will give you so much more room for creativity, and when you find something you love at a salvage yard or antique market you know you can snap it up and find a new use for it somewhere – a pile of fruit crates can house your library of books or CDs, a worn-out wardrobe fits in the kitchen next to a shiny stainless-steel fridge and finds a new life as a larder. Bits and pieces that are unloved and abandoned can be rescued, repaired and welcomed into your home – if you find a table with a broken leg tucked away in a dusty corner, wipe it clean and invite it in. Give it a new leg that doesn't match; if it's not the right height then all the better – even it up by adding some casters. Not being ruled by perfection means you can play around in this way, your things become customized and personal, and can share your sense of humour.

Taking furniture out of context gives your home an unexpected air, adds to the all-important element of contrast and allows you to have a sense of fun with what you do. Break the rules: bring garden furniture in from the cold and into your living space. Industrial bits rescued from redundant factories add a functional edge to your home; factory trolleys make great storage on wheels, ideal for almost everything from piles of fluffy towels to the contents of your organic veg box. Play around with what lighting goes where – articulated anglepoise lamps, along with grandly sparkling chandeliers, work in any room in the house, together or alone – just give them the chance to shine. Even broken bits of architrave or skirting board have a potential purpose. Combine them with bits of discarded floorboard to make an unusual mirror or picture frame, or use them to make a blocky stool that doubles as a bedside table. The list could go on and on!

Above all, if there is the faintest glimmer of life in something, rescue it – you're bound to be able to find a use for it somewhere. Think of your home as a delicious experiment.

elements

tones & textures

The decoration of the recycled home can't really be planned by poring over paint charts and choosing a mild-mannered colour scheme. Instead, be prepared to work with what you've got, and be open to the fun of discovering textural treasures that may have been covered up for years. Peel off layers of paint, plaster and dodgy wallpaper – at times you may start to feel a bit like a domestic archaeologist!

this page The wood blocks of this contemporary fire surround are ever so slightly different lengths, making them look as though they have been casually stacked around the fire. The wood is offcuts of floor- and skirting board, saved from a builder's bin and becoming firewood. The regularity of width provides a counterpoint to the heavily textured fireback as well as the wall behind, which is full of clues as to what it has been through.

opposite The plain fireplace surround is made from pieces of leftover green oak, rescued from a timber-framed house. Their clean-cut lines contrast perfectly with the roughness of the original fireplace, and the different hues of the weathered wood provide harmony between the fire and the peeled-back wall.

Decorating in this ever-so-slightly jumbled-up, back-to-front way makes it difficult to do too much advance planning, as you never really know what you will find. The diversity of textures to be uncovered in the home on large surfaces such as walls, floors and furniture and also in other, softer textiles provides you with the all-important element of contrast. This is the one principle you can plan around, to ensure you don't end up with an overwhelming mass of competing tones and textures – because you didn't know when to put down the paint scraper and take a step back.

Look for opportunities to introduce contrast. Think about what you put next to each other and how they can complement one another. A clean wall here and there or a pristinely white painted floor shows off the more textural areas brilliantly. Contrast is all about highlighting your best features,

thereby drawing attention to what's best about the best bits – allowing both elements to shine through.

Texture gives the recycled home a sense of character and the patina of age. Armed with scraper and sheets of sandpaper, carefully peel back the layers of paint and wallpaper left behind by previous owners. Like counting the rings of a tree, you can almost work out the age of a house by the decorating trends (or disasters) of the time. Stop when you find something you like – and be prepared for surprises. However, it is usually worth going back to the final layer; the exposed plasterwork with its patchwork of textures and soft chalky colours (and maybe a few remnants of something a bit brighter, depending on the colourful whims of earlier owners) is the perfect canvas for a room. Remember

this page Don't be afraid of imperfection. This cabinet rescued from a French hardware store may be missing a few drawers, but it is perfectly suited to its spot in a farmhouse kitchen. A piece of broken panelling becomes a work of art, which complements the textures and colours of the beautifully worn tiled floor.

ECROUX

COLLIERS

ATTACHES. CAPOTS.

KEEP AN EYE OUT FOR VINTAGE FINDS BUT DON'T ALWAYS ACCEPT THEM AT FACE VALUE. LOOK PAST A GAUDY PAINTED FINISH OR TOO-ORANGE VARNISH. STRIP PAINT OR VARNISH FROM CHESTS, CHAIRS, TABLES OR CUPBOARDS – GET BACK TO THE BASICS OF AN OBJECT.

to bear in mind the rule of contrast. If you don't want to be snowed under by too many different surfaces and scraps of colour then add contrast by perfectly plastering and painting one of the walls in a neutral shade of soft white. Alternatively, focus on the doors and skirting boards and let their newly revealed weathered qualities do the talking. If the walls are where the texture is, it's a good idea to provide contrast with smooth, clean-looking floors, such as white-painted wooden floorboards or more industrial-looking poured concrete. It's also much nicer for your feet!

Wooden panelling is another good way to introduce interest to a wall – mounting them horizontally rather than vertically prevents the Swedish sauna effect. Use recycled boards and experiment with different widths and hues of weathered wood. If you want something a bit less permanent or you live in a newer property, lean the boards against the wall as a way of framing a room. Old shop signs, pieces of moulded architrave and boards covered in paint drips and splashes also look great mixed in with plain planks, adding an extra textural twist. Wood gives a feeling of warmth, it looks natural and solid

above left Don't be overwhelmed by too many textures. Leave the floor clean-looking and perhaps one or two walls; with a fresh lick of white paint they will add breathing space. The heavily textured door, skirting board and the patchwork mirror frame stand out all the more in this light, airy dressing room.

above right A pile of deed boxes have been stripped of their black enamel paint and now have a soft sheen. The joy of undecoration is never quite knowing what you are going to find.

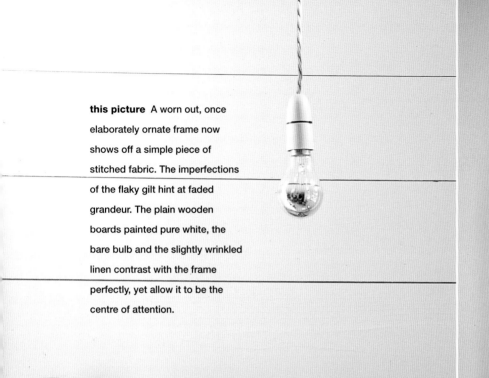

this picture A worn out, once elaborately ornate frame now shows off a simple piece of stitched fabric. The imperfections of the flaky gilt hint at faded grandeur. The plain wooden boards painted pure white, the bare bulb and the slightly wrinkled linen contrast with the frame perfectly, yet allow it to be the centre of attention.

above Painstakingly made from gently sandblasted offcuts of scaffolding board, which have been laminated together with their end grain on show, this unusual stairway looks unassumingly natural. The sparkling chandelier is the perfect choice of lighting as it is in total contrast to the simple stairs. However, the humorous addition of a hunk of driftwood to the chandelier ensures it doesn't get ideas above its station.

this page In this room the red, long forgotten Victorian child's sock provides a splash of colour. A battered but once grand gilt frame makes an ideal contrast to humble found objects. The combination also shows a keen sense of humour. A hairy twist of vine sits surprisingly well with the frame, the Arts and Crafts table and Regency chair – it all adds to the sense of the unexpected in this quiet corner.

in the face of dappled walls covered in peeling paint, and happily it gets better with time. Weathered wood battered by the elements and bleached by the sun always looks great and is reminiscent of holidays by the sea.

Recycled pieces of wood can be employed in many ways. Rescued floorboard offcuts that have already served their time underfoot make a great fireplace, and work well with either scraped-back or smooth walls. Wood has a timeless quality, so don't paint it. If you discover some useful wood that has been painted, try your best to remove the paint – but don't take away all traces of it, a few flaky remnants give a sense of what has been. Don't varnish your wooden finds either – how many shiny trees have you seen? The one thing you can treat your recycled wooden finds to is a spot of sandblasting, for an extra-weathered finish.

Texture can also be introduced with pieces of furniture. Keep an eye out for vintage finds but don't always accept them at face value. Look past a gaudy painted finish or too-orange varnish and consider what you could have on your hands if you

LIKE COUNTING THE RINGS OF A TREE, YOU CAN ALMOST WORK OUT THE AGE OF A HOUSE BY THE DECORATING TRENDS (OR DISASTERS) OF THE TIME. BE PREPARED FOR SURPRISES.

opposite Reveal the history of your home by peeling back its layers of paint. This door has been stripped in stages to reveal many different colours of paint. The most recent coat was a layer of white, followed by red, then blue, with the green paint being the oldest. The door has been honestly patched with a strip of copper.

above This door has been stripped in a more uniform way. The overall impressionistic greyish colour allows the door to gently stand out from the honey-coloured hues of the walls. The wires of the lighting system have been left on show, which fits in perfectly with the rawness of the recycled look.

remove them. Strip paint or varnish from chests, chairs, tables or cupboards – reveal what lies beneath and get back to the basics of an object. The recycled home is all about the honesty and integrity of materials, so don't cover things up or gloss over them: undecorate instead.

If you can't find what you want (or what you could use) by rummaging through markets, consider

opposite Here the natural beauty of wood is shown off to a tee. A screen made of scaffolding boards separates bedroom from bathroom. They were gently sandblasted to raise the grain, then lightly whitewashed. The skirting boards were treated in the same way to give the room a sense of cohesion. Scaffolding boards can also be spruced up with wire brushing and elbow grease if you don't fancy sandblasting.

WOODEN PANELLING IS A GOOD WAY TO INTRODUCE INTEREST TO A WALL – MOUNTING THEM HORIZONTALLY PREVENTS THE SAUNA EFFECT.

this page Smooth textures are as important as the more worn ones. Here, clean painted boards give a serene feel to a room. Next to the simple fireplace with its dark interior, they give a graphic black-and-white look, enhanced by the plainly framed photograph and the casually tucked-in postcard.

commissioning or making furniture out of recycled wood – floor- or scaffolding boards work well for most things. Ask a friendly building merchant what plywood offcuts he has lying around. Floorboards and skirting boards combined with scrap pieces of moulded architrave make great patchwork frames for mirrors, or could make a simple box-shaped stool that doubles up as a bedside table. If you've acquired an unloved chest of drawers with bits missing, fill in the gaps with a patchwork drawer or two. Put a mixture of old and new rescued wood together and see what happens – recycled furniture works best when it doesn't match and it is a good way of using every single bit of what you've got or what other people would throw away (making it good value for money, too).

Don't forget more modern, shiny surfaces; their smoothness complements more time-worn pieces. Metal furniture, trunks and crates benefit from a spot of undecoration too. If you're lucky enough to find painted boxes or lacquered trunks, remove the paint and you get a lovely scratchy, faded metallic surface, the perfect counterpoint to a flaky wall or chipped wooden cupboard.

Another way to introduce texture into your home is with pieces of art, whether paintings or three-dimensional works. Buy them from up-and-coming artists at graduation shows, or get your kids to help – brightly coloured drawings with wonky outlines go well with recycled textures and gentle tones. If you're feeling creative yourself, try making more abstract paintings on wooden boards that recreate the effect of a stripped-back wall. This is especially good if your house is a bit newer than you'd like, or if you can't be too heavy-handed with the walls – or if you want to practise your stripping skills first.

opposite The variety of textures in this kitchen harmonize as they are all of a similar hue, and are gently balanced by the green-painted door. The room has an honesty to it, as its faded, slightly worn-out aspects are unmasked.

above A scratchy child's drawing crayonned onto the back of an old panel saves the room from austerity and adds humour. An abandoned bit of balustrade becomes an unusual lamp base, topped off with a shade of French linen.

storage

Storage seems to be something we forever need more of. No matter how hard we try, there is always too much stuff requiring a home. Recycled storage is definitely not a case of buying more uniform flat-pack shelving: anything that requires an Allen key for assembly is out! What you do need is to be able to recognize the potential of an object. Recycled storage is all about giving something old and forgotten a new purpose.

left Use every inch of space you can lay your hands on, even if you have to climb a ladder to get to it. Here rolls of paper and old maps have been sneakily stored in the space between the top of a cupboard and the ceiling.

below Keep your room clutter free. There are some things that you just don't want on display. Hide them behind sleek wooden panelled doors to keep a serene atmosphere in your bedroom.

opposite Wake up 'dead' space by clever use of hooks and out-of-the-way high shelves hung from wooden beams. Employ battered old boxes and mesh bags to clear away things you don't use often.

When you are endeavouring to clear up your clutter and feel more organized, opt for recycled storage rather than buying something purpose-built and unimaginative. Look past the original purpose of an older object and consider how it could be the answer to your storage prayers. Rescued finds such as old wooden boxes, crates, fishermen's baskets, trunks and old factory trolleys are incredibly versatile and full of character. They are often printed with faded brand names or old logos, which add to the sense of history. For larger storage solutions, old shop fittings or medical cabinets are perfect when relocated into the kitchen, bathroom or bedroom. Do the decent thing, rescue them from the scrap heap and mould them to your own purpose. With

INDUSTRIAL STORAGE SUCH AS SHOE TROLLEYS MAKES GREAT OPEN SHELVING FOR JUST ABOUT ANYTHING. THEIR SLIGHTLY STARK, FUNCTIONAL FEEL – FLAKY PAINTED WOODEN SHELVES ON A METAL FRAME – MEANS THEY WORK WELL IN THE KITCHEN OR BATHROOM.

above left Old trolleys should have just about enough space for even the most avid collector of shoes and boots.

above centre A metal rack once used to house deed boxes now functions perfectly in the kitchen as domestic storage for pots, pans and old baskets.

above right Soften the hard-edged functionality of industrial storage trolleys. Stack them high with piles of clean towels and freshly laundered bed linen.

opposite An abandoned trolley rescued from an out-of-work shoe factory has been restored as a home for fashionable footwear. The wall behind the trolley bears the subtle traces of pattern imprinted from a piece of wallpaper long since removed.

such wonderful things waiting to be rediscovered and given a new lease of life, recycled storage merges into a display as you become more selective about what to have on show and what to stow away in old trunks, baskets or vintage suitcases.

If you are choosing the display-as-storage option, a bank of old fruit crates make great shelving. Piled on top of one another or fixed to a wall they unexpectedly become a recycled form of modular storage – use as many as it takes to fill your space and house your stuff. If you have the space, a whole wall of them can look amazing. In fact, crates are multi-talented in the world of storage; attach some casters and you've got moveable storage – with a magazine rack on wheels, you hardly need to rouse yourself from the sofa to pass the Sunday travel supplement!

Every now and then it's good to reuse something as it was designed. Old bottle crates for wine or fizzy drinks are fairly easy to get hold of and it doesn't take a great leap of imagination to work out what to do with them. Slightly altering their purpose will make them ideal storage for your glass recycling. Again, if you want your crates flexible, just add wheels.

Industrial storage such as shoe trolleys rescued from an old factory makes great open shelving for just about anything. Their slightly stark, functional feel – flaky painted wooden shelves on a metal frame – means they work well in the kitchen for piles of pots and pans or attractively packaged foodstuffs, or can be equally at home in the bathroom, ripe for softening with piles of fluffy towels. Or you could simply domesticate their original function and display your shoe collection.

Books always seem to spiral out of control, piles of them requiring more and more precious shelf space. Be creative with your library – plain ladderlike bookshelves made using rescued wooden boards for both the frame and shelves look good, and can easily be tailored to your collection's needs. They are also reminiscent of old-fashioned libraries, where ladders were required to get to the dusty volumes on the top shelf. While books multiply, so do music and film collections. Soften their plastic boxes by lining them up on wooden shelves with imperfect rough edges, or house them in a more industrial-chic style in old trunks or deed boxes, which can be piled on top of each other in size order. Alternatively, perch them on spindly metal legs made from scrap metal. Old metal drawers that have lost their filing cabinets or wooden ones missing their chests make handy storage too, and housed on top of a simple wooden table are much more flexible since becoming homeless!

If you have a spare bit of wall in an awkward corner or hallway, put up some hooks, but don't opt for the obvious; creative hooks include small pieces of driftwood, old shoe lasts or rescued old curly hooks. If you have a bag-collecting habit, make use of it by storing things in them at the same time.

Larger storage solutions come in the form of abandoned shop fittings, medical cabinets or lockers rescued from schools and universities. They can be used anywhere in the house and their generously appointed space makes them extremely useful. An extra-large old wardrobe, while useful in the bedroom, can also be used in the kitchen as a larder. Still in the kitchen, a shop counter makes an excellent work surface. Roomy old cupboards or refitted wardrobes also make excellent spaces to

opposite above left Past their sell-by date, these scaffolding boards with untrimmed ends have the appearance of driftwood, and work well as simple matching bookcases in this light and airy room.

opposite below left Who would have thought it – a rescued wooden pallet makes a perfect plate rack. Its rusty nails were left intact, and simply bent to keep the collection of plates in place. Its unassuming nature ensures the plates remain the focus of attention.

this page Salvaged wooden boards were used to make these deceptively simple, ladderlike bookshelves. Attention to detail is the key to this storage system – thin sheets of steel were carefully inserted to hold the books in place and the boards are held together at top and bottom with steel bands.

left A bank of reclaimed college lockers makes uniform storage in this kitchen. You could devise a labelling system, perhaps a tag hanging from each key, so that you're not constantly hunting high and low for what you need.

below These tin deed boxes, stripped of paint but unpolished, are bolted onto steel legs to make a CD store. Their solidity contrasts with the spindly mirror stand, an old hat-shop fitting. The fireplace surround includes recycled glass.

hide away some of life's entertainment necessities such as the inevitable televisions, DVD players and stereos. The chipped wood and imperfect surfaces of rescued furniture balance well with the sleekness of these machines, if you're leaving them on show. Glass-fronted metal medical cabinets are ideal for displaying smaller cherished items, and any personal collections amassed over time.

In the bedroom, it isn't necessary to hide your clothes away in a wardrobe, and it can be good to have them on display – you notice when a former favourite shirt hasn't been worn for a while and should be added to the charity-shop pile. Old trunks also make excellent storage for clothes. Have the current season's collection hanging out on display and easily accessible, and pack the rest carefully away. Trunks can be stripped of paint or ugly faux leather coatings – it just takes a bit of time and a lot of patience. Old suitcases and trunks are also a good place to stash away the things you don't need to get your hands on very often, such as skiwear or important paperwork that you need to keep but don't want to be permanently reminded of.

opposite below Old bottle
crates make useful storage
anywhere in the house and
are happily employed to
hold wine or your recycling.
Wheels make them mobile
and even more handy.

this page An interesting collection of wooden boxes
makes neat and classy-looking storage for paperwork.
Set on a simple trestle table they become a display
in their own right. On the shelf below, a decorative
embossed leather case stores hidden treasures
while being something of a talking point itself.

walls & floors

Walls and floors are your home's backdrop, setting the scene for everything else. Floors need to feel comfortable. Think about how good it feels to wander barefoot over a lawn or sandy beach – feet are sensitive, so treat them to something good. On walls you can get away with more. Layers of paint peeled back to chalky plasterwork feel wonderfully calm, even with the odd bit of flamingo wallpaper or turquoise paint left by a previous occupant.

left An ancient French tiled floor has been allowed to bask in the glory of its age rather than being replaced in favour of a younger, smoother model. It shows signs of wear but has been cared for over the years with beeswax polish.

right The walls and floors in this hallway have been left unadorned and simply mended where necessary. The flagstone floor shows where sturdy boots have tramped across it, but this adds character. Live with what you've got, and don't rush to replace it with something new and faceless.

Lift up your carpet and see what lies beneath. If you're really lucky, you'll find floorboards that simply require a spot of elbow grease to remove any paint remnants or just to give them a general clean. The next step is to consider the room – if it's a bit on the dark side, lighten it by giving your floorboards a lick of fresh white paint. This will also provide contrast if your walls are heavily textured. Painted boards are especially becoming in the bathroom as they give a feeling of cleanliness and calm, and claw-footed rolltop baths suit the look of old boards, quite literally, down to the ground.

If lifting your carpets is a disappointing exercise, then don't despair immediately. If at all possible work with what you've got – repair and recycle before you decide to rip up the whole thing and start again. In the past, mouse holes in floorboards were mended with pieces of old biscuit tin or baking trays. Revive this tradition – it lends extra character to your floor and is certainly cheaper than new boards. It is quite likely that you will have to lift your floorboards to reroute cables or pipes, so if larger areas of floor need repairing, now is the perfect time to do it. Replace rotten or wormy wood with pieces cut from other old boards. This patchwork effect looks perfect in the recycled home. If woodworm is a worry it can be treated, but be selective and only treat the areas that really need attention, as the sprays involved are toxic. Happily, it's quite likely that the majority of woodworm in old houses will already have left the building.

If you have to buy replacement flooring, look out for boards that have recently been lifted and denailed, rather than machined boards that have been cut from joists, as the latter don't have nail holes. In addition, recut boards don't have the same character as rescued

ones. However, you will need to be dedicated in your search for old flooring, as there are sadly no longer plentiful reserves of reclaimed boards around.

Stone and tiled floors are often found in heavy-traffic areas such as hallways and kitchens. They reveal more of the history of your home; elaborately decorative Victorian tiled entrances were all about making a good impression, and are still striking today. If you do have flagstone flooring or old tiles, then you've got a friend for life. Such floors last a very long time and age beautifully as you wear away a well-trodden path through your house. If your tiles need a bit of TLC, use a beeswax polish as it allows the tiles to breathe and you are less likely to end up with damp patches from trapped moisture. Above all, don't be afraid to leave a wonky flagstone or tiled floor alone. If your furniture gets a bit seasick, use wedges to even things up. Old cotton reels are especially suited to this task.

Textured walls go hand in hand with recycled, repaired patchwork flooring, and again the watchword is contrast – if your floor is heavily textured or very patchworked, keep the walls quite simple, maybe just having extra texture on doors and skirting boards. Obviously the

opposite above left A broken piece of cornice has been saved and highlights the lovely crumbly textures of a windowsill. It is almost like a miniature Grecian ruin.

opposite above right A modern chair is the perfect match in colour to this corner of peeled-back wall. Its graphic modernity is also an ideal counterpoint to the abstract patterns created by the different tones of the wall.

opposite below A table full of weird and wonderfully juxtaposed objects is set off perfectly by the beautiful colours of the exposed plasterwork. The harmonious tones of wall and objects give the room an air of restful contemplation; it becomes a dreamlike museum or gallery space.

this page An industrial articulated light adds a utilitarian edge to the softness of the slightly pink tones in this wall. The exposed wooden beam ensures the area retains a natural warmth.

opposite The flaky brickwork and paint around this hearty fireplace are an extreme example of the undecorated look. The framed pictures and casually arranged postcards give the room a lived-in feel. The lighter areas around the fire show the effect of damp as the fire draws moisture higher up the wall.

this page If you don't want to live with such extremes, create smaller, more user-friendly areas of texture. Here layers of paper and paint are combined to create a dramatic artwork, which reflects the peeling layers of the room opposite. Its pride of place on a clean, smooth wall emphasizes its textures all the more.

this page Combinations of materials left behind by previous generations work beautifully together. Stone and tiled floors were used in areas of heavy human traffic such as entrances, pantries and kitchens, as they could stand up to the wear and tear of constant visitors. Wooden floors were usually found in living areas as they provided a feeling of luxury and warmth. Today they combine perfectly with the faded grandeur of exposed walls and doors and pieces of handmade furniture.

TEXTURED WALLS GO HAND IN HAND WITH RECYCLED, REPAIRED PATCHWORK FLOORING, AND AGAIN THE WATCHWORD IS CONTRAST – IF YOUR FLOOR IS HEAVILY TEXTURED, KEEP THE WALLS QUITE SIMPLE, MAYBE HAVING EXTRA TEXTURE ON DOORS AND SKIRTING BOARDS.

above left Sometimes the colours left behind are too lovely to get rid of. Here a gorgeous chalky blue limewash has been allowed to stay. With its slight flaws and imperfections, it fits in with the grand scheme of the undecorated house. It also goes well with the grey flagstone flooring and multi-toned, exposed original plaster walls.

above right Natural textiles such as this sacking and string, now used as a simple bag, are an ideal companion to exposed walls and floors. They have an unassuming grace that speaks of harder times past, and almost seem to thank you for the chance to rest!

opposite is also true – textured walls seem somehow easier to live with if the floors are impressively clean and white.

If you do choose to decorate by taking things away rather than adding new layers of paint, you get to see what decorating highs and lows your house has been through – it's a bit like carbon dating your house as you uncover layer upon layer of colour and tone. What is finally exposed can be gently beautiful, as the changing colours and papers of the past can't help but leave behind a faint impression of what once was. Also if elements such as wooden panelling, cables, or dado or picture rails were removed from your rooms by previous owners, then you get an extra dimension of tone to your peeled-back walls as these former features leave behind subtle alterations in colour. Delicate differences can also be seen around fireplaces as heat draws moisture up the walls.

Limewashing is a good old-fashioned alternative to paint; thin layers of limewash have a delicious textured matt finish and chalky pastel paleness. Not only do they look good, but their permeability allows walls to breathe, which reduces the risk of damp. Old limewashed walls must be treated with consideration and should only be decorated with another limewash layer, as modern emulsion would simply blow off.

this page The walls of this room, with their dotty texture, are strangely reminiscent of ostrich leather. The owner of this space managed to stop the architect from covering up these beautiful walls just in time. The strange marks were actually made for keying the wall ready for replastering. The extra-large articulated lamp spotlights a worn old sign warning of the dangers of fire – just above the fireplace!

ATTENTION au FEU

this page Again the mixture of wood and tiled flooring, relics of the past, has been kept on show. The stairs show signs of previous carpet and the geometrically patterned encaustic tiles show the skill of Victorian workmen (they were laid without any grout). An oversized garden spade from an old hardware store makes an immediate comic impact on entrance to this house. It seems even larger placed as it is near a child-sized tailor's dummy.

lighting

Lighting is all about creating an atmosphere, and its importance in making your home a comfortable and inviting place shouldn't be underestimated. Recycling in the lighting world means throwing out the rule book. All sorts of lamps and lights can look great transplanted from, say, a building site or even a chicken shed into your bedroom or home office. Recycled lighting tends towards the industrial, but often with an unexpected twist.

AN OLD INSPECTION LAMP WITH ITS WIRE CAGE, PLACED ON A BEDSIDE TABLE, FEELS SIMPLE, HONEST, AND PERFECTLY IN KEEPING WITH THE RECYCLED HOME AESTHETIC.

Forward planning is perhaps the most important thing when introducing lighting into your home, especially if you're rewiring the entire house. This early stage is an opportunity to decide exactly what you want and where you want it, so think about your lighting needs; different activities require different kinds of lighting. Don't forget sockets. Plan for one or two more than you think you're going to need.

Often an odd mix of lights, lamps and wall lights does a better job than one central light trying desperately to illuminate a room right into the murkiest corners. So think about lighting in groups – this way you get to be a bit more energy-efficient as well, because you can go for lower-wattage bulbs.

A simple row of old-fashioned filament lightbulbs hung from twisted corded flex makes excellent lighting for a lengthy hallway or hung over a long canteen-style dining table. Use extra flex, then you can easily adjust the height by tying a loose knot. These hanging bulbs also look great suspended on extra-long cord over a bedside table, or slung over a nail to make a minimal wall light. The bare bulbs lose their austere, institutional feel when you choose this kind of flex instead of the unattractive PVC sort. It is available in silver, bronze, black or gold and hangs beautifully. Regardless of the style of bulbs you decide on, choose clear rather than pearl and definitely avoid those with a hint of a tint of colour.

A rewired French inspection lamp cage, rescued from a former life in a chicken shed, gives an industrial edge and can be gainfully employed in a number of ways.

opposite left The shiny, skinny steel of the hanging wire contrasts with the no-nonsense functionality of the lamp cage.

opposite right This bedroom is converted to the industrial look with simple furniture made from recycled materials, such as the Meccano®-like table topped with scaffolding board and the scaffolding-pole bed. Pure white linen completes the theme.

this page The lamp is given a slightly softer feel with a driftwood base. Corded flex trailing along the floor hangs beautifully – much better than ugly PVC.

lighting

59

elements

On the poster: VIOLET S[...] / CHARLOTTENB[...] / 15 · 30 april 1978 / daglig 10 · 17 fri o[...]

opposite A rescued operating-theatre lamp casts a bright light over this draughtsman's table. Its multi-mirrored surface ensures it is more electricity friendly than might initially appear, requiring only one bulb to shine. The cupboards were rescued from a university science block, so are appropriately in keeping with the medical theme.

this page, clockwise from left A 1950s Italian lamp brightens a dark corner. An anglepoise lamp with a spun stainless-steel shade has been removed from its original home on a workbench and used as a flexible wall lamp. A classic-style bike lamp is given a new function on an old lamp base; two unloved pieces come together to make a great-looking, unexpected lamp with a quirky sense of fun.

below An articulated industrial light is perfectly positioned over a painting as an unusual, unobtrusive spotlight.

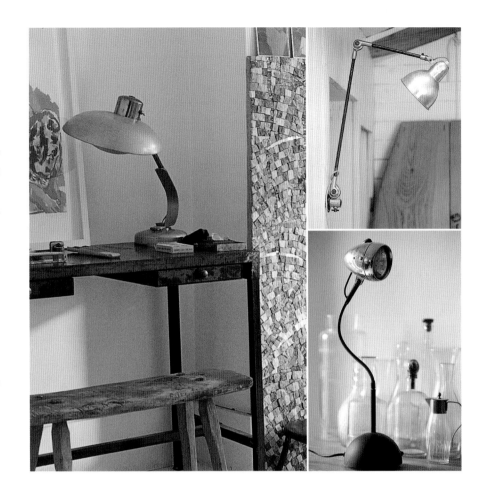

If you want more than bare bulbs, be creative with your choice of shade. All manner of recycled finds can be used, such as old kilner jars, which can be adapted into lovely hanging lamps that are perfect for the kitchen. Just remember that you are dealing with electricity, so it's best to plan your designs and then get a qualified electrician to turn them into reality. Other options if you want to unleash your creative capabilities are lights, desperate for rescue, that were designed for a specific function and are no longer needed. Again, ask an electrician to adapt them to your needs. Workmen's lamps, or even lamps rescued from a chicken shed, can work wonderfully in the home. If an old inspection lamp with its wire cage feels like a step too far, it can be softened with a driftwood base or suspended from a spindly stainless-steel wire. Placed on or above a bedside table it feels simple, honest and perfectly in keeping with the recycled home aesthetic.

Rescued anglepoise lamps look great, especially if you give them time out of the office and allow them into the rest of your home. They come in a variety of styles and colours and their angular adaptability makes them perfect for reading by, lighting pictures or brightening a dark corner. When you are rescuing an old anglepoise, remember it is unlikely to be earthed, so you will need to have the wiring checked or replaced.

If industrial lighting feels too stark, a rescued standard lamp with a tasselled shade provides a good contrast. Bring it up to date by painting the stand and then carefully semi-removing the paint, or by wrapping the stand in scraps of vintage fabric. Chandeliers are a glamorous counterbalance to industrial lights. They may need a spot of refurbishment or a replacement drop or two. Chandeliers give a delicate twinkling light and an air of decadence and old-world charm, ideal in recycled rooms with their chalky textured walls. Don't restrict them to the living room either – chandeliers add instant chic to a bathroom or kitchen.

this page Dolly switches are so satisfying to use. Old ones in ceramic or Bakelite can still be tracked down, but old-style, new versions are a safer bet.

opposite Make a statement in your shed. An old Sputnik light makes a dramatic centrepiece. Its industrial bare bulbs are complemented by the simple table made with Dexion® legs (usually seen as shelving) and an array of mismatched designer chairs.

this page Old standard lamps can still look good if you treat them to a makeover. Enhance their frilly, flowery nature and wrap the stand in scraps of vintage fabric. They work well with uncomplicated furniture. The owner of this bed has extended the DIY look of the lamp to the bed by attaching braid to its headboard and end, uniting the two disparate pieces.

opposite A tasselled vintage shade adds a splash of colour.

opposite inset above Celebrate over-the-top florals. Put them together in a friendly group and they provide balance and humour to liven up a plain-painted room.

opposite inset below A rewired chandelier is given a quirky twist with the addition of a chunky piece of driftwood.

IF INDUSTRIAL LIGHTING FEELS TOO STARK, A RESCUED STANDARD LAMP WITH A TASSELLED SHADE PROVIDES A GOOD CONTRAST. BRING IT UP TO DATE BY WRAPPING THE STAND IN VINTAGE FABRIC.

Flickering candlelight is another way to soften industrial lighting. Keep an eye out for battered, unloved candlesticks and candelabras and welcome them into your home. Again, other, more unexpected objects can make excellently quirky candle holders; for example, you could wrap wire around the rim of a jam jar and hang it from a hook.

Of course where you've got lighting you'll need switches. Old-style dolly switches look so much better than square white plastic ones. If you find old ceramic or Bakelite switches, get them checked and reconditioned before using them. Don't despair if you can't find any, because new, reproduction dolly switches are available.

display

The principles of recycling go hand in hand with collecting and consequently display. Seeing the beauty and potential in an abandoned object, rescuing it and taking it home can become a habit, and before you know it you have a collection. If you love something enough to preserve it then you're bound to want to show it off, so consider display options. Look for a link – materials, colour or items from the same place or time.

above Recessed shelving painted glossy bright white provides the perfect display area for a mix of rescued pieces. Limiting the colours of this collection to black and white creates a bold, graphic statement.

below This collection of old brown Betty china teapots is housed in sympathetic wooden crate shelving.

opposite Domestic bazaar! All sorts of odds and ends are brought together on a bleached Indian daybed, quirkily converted into a table and finished with a shoe-last foot. The mirror frame is made from an old cog, and the huge last was found in an Italian shoe factory.

Display in the recycled home shouldn't cost lots of money – it isn't necessarily about spending thousands on a fancy cabinet or a painting that matches your cushions. A haphazard mix of items built up over years of trawling through markets, travelling or beachcombing is much more interesting, because it is personal. The objects you've collected remind you of past adventures and have a story to tell. Displaced from their original surroundings, this story becomes all the more poignant.

Displays work best when a little bit of thought has gone into them. An odd mixture of objects, from delicate pottery to chipped and chunky print blocks to an old cycle helmet, can work wonders together if they are grouped according to colour. The same goes for objects made of similar materials – scraps of driftwood mixed with balls of string and wooden beads make an eye-catching and harmonious display. Rusty-round-the-edges shop signs or ex-marketing display items such as an extra-large shoe last, huge pencil or child-sized spoon and fork give a display an extra twist. A weird item thrown into the mix makes you look twice and appreciate the display even more.

Treasures picked up while travelling in foreign climes, such as ethnic-looking pottery, woven hats, pebbles or shells look great displayed in small gangs, maybe with a group for each holiday if you have the space. If travel is your thing, a mixed-up arrangement of old globes perched on

this page A retired circular saw bench is given the chance to show off its industrial good looks. It now proudly displays a collection of African vases and pottery.

opposite left An old stone kitchen fireplace is the resting place for this intriguing group. The monkeys were found in a falling-apart book and framed so as not to be forgotten.

Beads hang from a hook, which was part of a gun rack – these were traditionally found above fireplaces to keep the guns dry.

opposite right Group small framed pictures with similar colours or themes together to create one large artwork.

a shelf can help you decide on your next destination. Old maps showing obsolete or bypassed routes, or long-sent postcards, look good patchworked over the door of an ugly fridge, or you could indulge your wanderlust and paper an entire wall with them.

Think about what you display your objects in or on. Smaller things, maybe abandoned strips of pearly buttons, tape measures or old needles still in their packets rescued from a closed-down haberdashery, look good housed in old glass jars lined up along a shelf. A collection of bright retro glass vases looks best on a window ledge – as the sun shines in, their vibrant colours really sing out. Use sympathetic recycled display materials, such as old wooden seed trays or small wooden crates. Give cheap and cheerful objects an elevated museum-like feel by placing them in old glass-fronted medical cabinets, second-hand fish tanks or large glass vases. In this way they become reminiscent of artworks by the American artist Joseph Cornell, whose odd collaged objects trapped in wooden boxes tell strange tales.

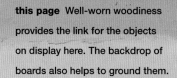

this page Well-worn woodiness provides the link for the objects on display here. The backdrop of boards also helps to ground them.

opposite A bright example of using colour to bring together a disparate collection. Even the wall is painted to highlight the display. The lustre of the glass vase provides just the contrast required by the more rough and ready bits.

AN ODD MIXTURE OF OBJECTS, FROM DELICATE POTTERY TO CHUNKY PRINT BLOCKS, CAN WORK WONDERS GROUPED TOGETHER BY COLOUR.

Another way to display your favourite things is to hang them. Use strategically placed hooks looped with fishermen's thread or skinny stainless-steel wire. A lonely children's shoe, which lost its partner long ago, makes a striking sculptural statement this way. Hang a blank luggage tag from it and leave the viewers to make up the story for themselves. Old glass beads sparkle when hung from simple hooks, and stay tidy into the bargain. If you've got a beautiful vintage dress, don't hide it away, hang it from an old-fashioned coat hanger or track down an abandoned tailor's dummy, another good way of displaying favourite clothes and keeping your jewellery neat.

Some old objects that seem to have lost their way in life could be given a new job to do if you think about them from a different angle. A rescued shoe last makes a handy incense holder, or you could attach a utility clip and turn it into an informal picture holder. If you find a lovely old teapot but its lid is missing, bring it home anyway and use it as a vase.

Displays of recycled objects can be ever-changing because the artefacts are not necessarily family heirlooms which have to be locked away. Much of the fun of display comes from such flexibility. You can have a host of rescued objects ready to be rearranged on a whim. It keeps your home feeling fresh and interesting and it is certainly a cheaper way of updating your surroundings than redecorating – and so much more fitting for the recycled way of life.

textiles

Textiles are an easy way to bring recycling into your home. The endless uses for small or large pieces of rescued fabrics embody the principles of recycling – adapt, repair and reuse. Textiles are also perfect for softening the sometimes hard edges of other recycled elements. A cushion on a wirework garden chair transplanted to your kitchen table or a patchwork bedspread thrown onto a roughly hewn oak bed make comfortable contrasts.

When you come across inspiring vintage fabrics in charity shops, specialist antique linen shops or at a vintage fabric fair, a whole world of possibilities opens up before you. Remember, before you get too carried away with crafty ideas, to take a step back and thoroughly inspect your potential purchase. There's little point in entertaining thoughts of a whole suite of new cushions if the fabric unfolds to reveal it was once a generous supper to a horde of hungry moths, has faded in the sunlight or is stained with difficult-to-remove rust. It may well still be useful, but perhaps not for what you first imagined.

CUSHIONS COVERED IN A VARIETY OF TICKINGS SIT WELL TOGETHER PILED HIGH ON A SQUASHY SOFA, BUT IF YOU LIKE A FEW CLASHING COLOURS CHOOSE A BRIGHT COLOUR NEXT TO A VIVID GEOMETRIC PATTERN.

If you decide to repair a rescued piece of vintage fabric, then don't be too precious about it. Show your work – uneven simple sewing, blanket stitch and really obvious seams have personality and are just right for the recycled home – and they're much easier to achieve than perfect invisible mending!

Rescued textiles come into all areas of the home. Keep things uncomplicated, then it is much easier to mix and match. Cushions covered in a variety of different tickings sit well together piled

opposite above An old lace tablecloth has been given a new purpose as a simple curtain. Its sheer quality really comes into its own here, diffusing a soft light into the room.

opposite below Cushions covered in different-coloured tickings sit well together – the simplicity of the pattern makes it easy to mix and match. The addition of a fringed blanket to the casually covered sofa makes it a welcoming nest.

this page Striped fabric matching the direction of the wooden panelling adds to the serene, beach-like feel of this room.

this page Fabric rescued from an old bathing tent makes a simple pair of honestly mended curtains.

opposite left Woollen blankets make warm winter curtains – but keep in mind that it's not always easy to find a matching pair (if matching is your thing).

opposite right Crocodile clips make an impromptu curtain holder and mean you don't damage your curtain fabric or linen tea towel.

high on a squashy sofa because they have similar characteristics, but if you like a few clashing colours here and there try sticking to fabrics from a similar period, or choose a bright colour next to a startlingly vivid geometric pattern. Sofa-wise, if you have one whose upholstery has seen better days then dust sheets make ideal throws as they're large enough to do the job and are a good neutral backdrop to other, more glamorous cushions and blankets. If you choose to have your sofa reupholstered in a range of complementary vintage pieces, then again show the honesty of the work by having the seams and joins on show and using big stitches. This form of dressing particularly suits sofas that are quite a fussy, decorative shape. Whatever you do, make sure your sofa is cosy, perhaps with extra rescued blankets on hand for cold winter evenings and lots of cushions covered in a patchwork of fabric finds.

opposite An unusual monochrome patchwork quilt, made from pieces of dyed denim stitched together, then occasionally patched. The irregular stitching is integral to the design of this deceptively haphazard-looking quilt.

this page An old shawl adds an extra layer to this cosy bed. The contrasting tablecloth was picked up in Uzbekistan. Black velvet shoes make a dramatic display on the mantelshelf.

You could even use old knitwear from charity shops, or any shrunken washday disasters! If you are feeling creative, track down old upholstery sample books and turn them into cushions or patches for your sofa too.

Curtains require larger areas of fabric, but if you can't find perfect pieces then roughly patch any holes or sew smaller pieces together. These imperfections give the curtains character and fit in with the other textiles found in the recycled home. Welsh blankets make warm winter curtains and can be swapped in summer for an old lace tablecloth that allows soft summer sunlight into your home. Similarly, old French linen tea towels make excellent curtains for small windows. Hang them straight up using crocodile clips, and you can keep your tea towels or tablecloths intact, meaning you can also use them elsewhere later. Beds are another ideal location for rescued fabric. Follow the original principle of patchwork and use scraps left over from cushion- or curtain-making.

Rugs are a good way of introducing textiles into your home, and in the recycled home they don't have to be perfect. Old kilims picked up abroad, when you couldn't say no to the man in the carpet shop, can

THE TINIEST PIECE OF FABRIC IS USEFUL AND CAN GIVE FUNCTIONAL FURNITURE A PERSONAL TWIST. WRAP REMNANTS CAREFULLY AROUND THE HANDLES ON A CHEST OF DRAWERS OR ON THE BUTTONS OF A CHAIR.

opposite Small fabric details make a big impact. They add a splash of colour and quirky visual interest as they unexpectedly catch your eye. They are an ideal way to use up scraps of vintage fabric, too. The owner of this classic Barcelona stool by Ludwig Mies van der Rohe (**below**) has personalized it by wrapping the buttons in brightly coloured scraps. It is a great way to customize a favourite piece of furniture (or even to perk up a less appealing item). It makes the piece well and truly yours, and unlike anything else.

top right Worn out kilims, cut up and stitched together, create a clever and unusual patchwork stair carpet.

above right A patchwork blanket uses up every last bit of fabric. This one softens the lines of an Edwardian steamer chair.

be chopped up and turned into beautiful patchwork rugs, their more ragged areas craftily hidden around the edges of the rug. (The same principle applies to any rug or scraps of rugs you find.)

By the time you've finished all these projects you may not be left with much in the way of fabric, but even the tiniest piece is useful and can give functional furniture a personal twist. Wrap remnants carefully around the handles on a chest of drawers or on the buttons of a chair. Small details such as these can make a big impact.

rooms

kitchens

Somehow everyone always ends up gathered in the kitchen. A kitchen made up of recycled elements is a relaxed space to gossip over a cup of coffee or prepare your Sunday lunch, so say no to the hard-edged uniformity of a fitted kitchen; free-standing pieces are much more versatile. All sorts of things can be used in the kitchen if you give your imagination free rein and forget long-held notions about the function of furniture.

opposite Mismatched chairs around a huge canteen table bring people together for informal dining. Plenty of plates and glasses are on hand in this French farmhouse kitchen, encouraging guests to help themselves. A suspended lamp is wrapped in an old linen cloth to soften the light.

right A well-worn but still perfectly usable larder provides a contrast with the more high-tech appliances in this kitchen. The pile of chopped wood also adds to the feeling of attracting opposites.

below A massive oak refectory table and bench are lit by contrasting fittings. An old candle chandelier hangs happily alongside a scalloped glass shade, setting the tone for this striking example of a recycled dining area. The wall of painted wooden panelling makes an impressive backdrop. Its horizontal lines were revealed when lath and plaster, which kept the beauty of the rare painted panelling hidden for years, was removed.

Consider what you need in your kitchen. Generally it will be acres of space to prepare your food and plenty of storage for pots, pans and plates as well as for bottles, boxes and teabags, then a table for the hungry hordes to sit at and devour their lovingly prepared meals, and maybe somewhere warm for the cat. Once you know what you need, get into the swing of creative thinking about what furniture lives where

IF YOU COME ACROSS AN OLD WARDROBE, SNAP IT UP. FITTED WITH A FEW SHELVES (OF RECYCLED WOOD OF COURSE), IT WILL MAKE A ROOMY LARDER.

and what its function is – this way everything has potential. The kitchen in the recycled home is not about creating a specific look. Rather, it is about a mixture of ideas, making good use of what you find and breaking rules about cupboards and work spaces.

If you come across an old wardrobe, snap it up. Transplanted into the heart of the home and fitted with a few shelves (of recycled wood of course), it will make a roomy larder. If it is painted, strip it back as you would your walls: crackled flaky surfaces are a lovely contrast to the kitchen's inevitably shiny stove and fridge. Old shop counters make spacious work surfaces for chopping and stirring, and what's more they come with plenty of built-in storage, either cupboards or drawers depending on the shop they

came from. Abandoned workbenches are also extremely useful. They are usually a generous size and perfect for an open-plan storage system – an unsystematic pick 'n' mix of pasta packets in enamel buckets alongside boxes of cereal stashed in willow baskets.

If you think something has potential, however down at heel it seems at first, accept the challenge. If the old shop counter you're considering for your kitchen feels a bit too grungy, then a stainless-steel or reclaimed slate worktop could be the answer and will be a great contrast to the well-worn wood. If it has lost a door or drawer, patch it with reclaimed boards or even strips of old blackboard; that way it's easy to remember what is squirrelled

above left A key element of the look is captured perfectly here in the contrast between the well-worn surfaces of an old wardrobe, reinvented as a larder, and a sleek modern fridge.

above right A new designer tap contrasts with a chunky Belfast sink. The entire kitchen sink stand was made from reclaimed planks.

left A vast wooden dresser displays an array of white china. Assorted chairs sit around a table lit by bare filament bulbs strung from twisted, corded flex.

opposite A worn shop counter makes a perfect kitchen island. The unintentional patchwork paint, chips and scratches give it a well-used feel. The lampshade and oven provide a modern contrast.

CYCLES

BULLS

this picture Wonderfully weathered old wooden shutters have been topped and tailed to make cupboard doors, which hide some of the less attractive kitchen essentials. The solid stone work surface is ideal for showing off wobbly piles of plates and dishes.

left A collection of old wooden chopping boards and different-sized pestles and mortars gathers around the sink.

below left Rusty bent nails keep the plates in position in this clever example of recycling – a rack, made from a pallet, to display a collection of unusual plates.

OPEN SHELVING GIVES YOU THE OPPORTUNITY TO DISPLAY COLLECTIONS OF PLATES, BOWLS OR GLASSES; A WONKY PILE OF CROCKERY LOOKS TOO GOOD TO HIDE BEHIND CUPBOARD DOORS.

away where. Above all, keep in mind the basic principles of the recycled home – reuse, repair and adapt before discarding anything.

For flexible kitchen storage, a scuffed 'work-in-progress' trolley rescued from a factory makes an ideal vegetable rack on wheels. Wire plimsoll lockers are a perfect place to store your wine, and shoe trolleys can hold piles of pots and pans. Open shelving gives you the opportunity to display collections of plates, bowls and glasses, or a wonky pile of crockery that looks too good to hide behind cupboard doors. This way everything is easily accessible. Favourite dishes can be displayed and stored in a wooden pallet hung on a wall. Old windows make excellent wall-hung cupboard fronts that allow you to display and protect from dust at the same time.

Saving money with recycled furniture should hopefully leave you with extra cash to spend on appliances that cannot be substituted with something older. Get the best you can afford, buy stand-alone fridges and dishwashers and remember to look for the most energy-efficient. Consider a professional stove. It will last a lifetime and be much sturdier than its domestic cousin. Industrial-looking catering equipment is often handily on wheels, so is flexible, and easy to pull out and clean around. Its no-nonsense, functional good looks and all-round sturdiness will sit nicely with the aged appearance of recycled finds. If you want an old stove, it is sometimes possible to find a good reconditioned one, but get it properly checked before you buy, as safety is paramount.

Chunky ceramic Belfast sinks are increasingly popular and can be found in good condition in salvage yards (it's worth remembering that the new ones are still made using traditional methods). They are beautifully functional as their extra-large dimensions give you more room to manoeuvre. They are well matched (or rather contrasted) with sculptural contemporary taps. Consider opting for hardwearing, efficient commercial taps. Those with an extendable hose are brilliant for all kinds

of kitchen chores. Old taps should probably be avoided as they will already have done their fair share of labour and you need them to last.

Once the fundamentals of your kitchen are in place (or if you have inherited a fitted kitchen and want to give it a bit of personality), the fun part of

opposite left Old college lockers suspended just above the floor provide a handy bank of storage in this open-plan kitchen made entirely of recycled finds.

opposite right, above and below A variety of hooks, some dating back to the 1950s, is a wonderful way of storing odd bits and bobs like elastic bands, which can never be found when you need them.

above right Take a tip from the professionals. A collection of old and new knives is stored safely on wall-mounted magnetic strips.

below right Stacked lockers provide more storage in this kitchen, where every inch has been employed to create a well-functioning space. An extendable ladder leads to further storage.

opposite above right and left
Wooden cupboards made from
sandblasted scaffold boards are
a good balance to industrial-style
kitchen fittings. Offcuts became a
wall-hung storage box for utensils.

opposite below left A table with
turned wooden legs and spindly
chairs adds a traditional twist.

opposite below right A chair has
been repaired the old-fashioned
way, using a small piece of tin.

this page and details opposite
A reclaimed wood table is topped
with contrasting thin steel. The
austerity of the table and bare bulb
is balanced by a mix of ornate and
weathered chairs, all reflected in
an enormous distressed mirror.

this page Rescued embossed American ceiling panels topped with smooth stainless steel create a beautiful counter. The floor is made from ground marble offcuts, granite and other waste materials. The polished countertop, the clean lines of the table and the industrial pendant light provide just the right amount of contrast.

opposite While these chairs are of a matching design, the rescued wooden planks used to construct them give each one an individual air. The old French industrial light adds a utilitarian twist, especially with the conduit on display.

filling it with rescued accessories and gadgets starts. Old kitchenware was generally well made and built to last, so there is lots of it just waiting to be rescued and welcomed into your home. The recycled kitchen is all about informality and mixing and matching rather than having a complete set of porcelain. An ornate silver fork makes a perfect partner to an eye-popping 1960s graphic print plate and is well stored along with its mismatched colleagues in an old glass confit jar. Attractive old mechanical coffee grinders with wooden drawers should still work if you find them, as there is so little that can go wrong. The same goes for old enamelware and milk bottles printed with the names of defunct dairies; they make plain vases just right for the recycled kitchen.

Dining should be relaxed and informal, not concerned with a pristine tablecloth and matching napkins. It's more about cramming as many people

this picture Open shelving is the perfect showcase for this collection of African pottery. The uneven piles of plates and bowls painted in earthy hues of yellow, green and gold look great next to the clean lines of the shelves and provide the main source of colour. The extra-thick work surface adds an industrial finish and works well with the utilitarian indoor barbecue.

inset The collection of white crockery and recycled glass is not as neat as it seems. The plates are handmade with delicate, wobbly edges and the hand-blown glass carafes lean as if a little bit tipsy.

above The recycled elements of this room lie in the subtle detail. This kitchen shows that a contemporary look can work perfectly as a backdrop for treasured collections. The distinct separation of the different collections, along with the white walls and seamless surface of the giant custom-built table, prevent the kitchen from feeling cluttered and provide an oasis of calm.

as possible around a huge canteen-style table. Get the biggest table you can fit into your space, even if it means knocking through into your dining room. An open-plan arrangement is much more sociable, and gives you someone to chat to while you stir the risotto. If you can't find a table big enough, buy two and graft them together. Hybrid tables fit perfectly into the recycled home way of doing things, and it means you have unlimited options when you are on your rescuing spree. If you find a beautiful, well-worn wooden table whose legs have seen better days, then transplant the top onto a different, sturdy base: if it doesn't match, so much the better! Alternatively, get a table made to suit your needs (and dimensions). Experiment with textures and materials, mix and match; use what you can find or salvage. Use floorboards as a tabletop, leaving the sawn edges so the grain is on show. Put a skinny

metal top on chunky wooden legs made from discarded scaffolding boards to create a table with surprising elegance.

As far as seating arrangements go, a mismatched collection of chairs looks best gathered around your refectory-sized table. It ends up looking rather like you've invited friends for supper with the proviso that they bring their own chair. They seem to get on well together – sensible wooden chapel chairs with loopy wirework garden ones, or classic French metal seats and stools mixed with a grand old-fashioned dining chair. As with the table, you can create your own chairs. Weathered oak blocks make stunning stools and provide a chunky contrast to a spindly four-legged friend. An industrial base, perhaps from a machinist's chair with an unusable seat, can be given a new lease of life with a simple wooden top. Pile them around your table, perhaps adding a few cushions made from vintage fabric, and you won't want to leave.

Lighting is important in the kitchen, it's one place where you really do need to see what you are doing! Large industrial hanging shades or old maritime shades made for ocean-going yachts and cargo ships are perfect for casting a glow over a wide area. Complement them with extra spotlights; anglepoise lamps work just as well here as they do in the office. As kitchen and dining areas increasingly merge together in our homes, two different lighting schemes are a necessity as you go from bright task lighting to more subtle lighting for dining. Bare filament bulbs hanging from a length of corded flex suit the functionality of the kitchen and are also effective hanging in a row over a long canteen table, especially if you can control them with a dimmer switch. Contrast them with an elaborate candelabra and dine in a relaxed, recycled atmosphere.

this page A rustic-style cabinet was cleverly constructed from scaffolding boards held in place with a long, sculptural pole (as well as one or two hidden pins and catches). The whole thing, with its collection of glass decanters and piles of plates, reflects the serenity of the still life hung behind it.

opposite Recycled materials can be used to create meticulously planned kitchens. This simple but well configured space was built using worn bricks, perfectly positioned to house a sleek dishwasher and stove, as well as more informal baskets for storage.

living rooms

The recycled living room is a long way from a stuffy formal reception room. It is a place to relax and feel comfortable, somewhere to unwind at the end of the day, be it curling up with a book or dancing round the sofa. It's a reflection of you, so you'll want sociable seating and storage. You need to feel you can kick off your shoes and not worry where they land.

All of the elements of the recycled home come together in the living room. Here mixed-up textures and textiles combine harmoniously, providing a feeling of relaxation and informality. The living room gives you an opportunity to assert your personality, because it is where you spend much of your leisure time. Everything should be easily accessible, but the room shouldn't feel too cluttered or you won't be able to relax. However, you do need a few places to display your personal treasures.

The sofa is the all-important hub of inactivity in the recycled living room. If you find an old sofa that needs rescuing, make sure you test it first. This doesn't require an expert, just take a seat and keep your fingers crossed that there are no stray springs poised to take you unawares! If you discover a good

opposite above left The attention to detail in the covering of this sofa means that even the turned legs are wrapped in vintage fabric. With its exposed edges and raw stitches, there is an honesty to this unusual upholstery: all its imperfections are proudly on show.

opposite above right Two huge sofas make a comfortable spot for basking in the sunshine filtering through floor-to-ceiling windows.

opposite below left Unfussy jute string was used to stitch the edges of this armchair, which has been covered in painted canvas.

opposite below right A French garden table has been transplanted into the living room. Its dainty curvy legs contrast beautifully with the sturdy sofa.

this page What could be quite a traditional room is given a subtle recycled home update with details such as the inside-out upholstery, the old saw bench in the corner and travel treasures on display.

left The recycled look makes for an informal, relaxing living room. The prominence of natural materials, raw edges and unfussy furnishings gives a serene feel. The 'cycles' sign is from a bike shop in the Welsh valleys, while the sculptural pieces on the fireplace are actually hat stands and a mounted watering-can rose.

right A bank of wooden crates makes a roomy bookcase and storage space.

IF YOU HAVE A FIREPLACE WITH A MISSING OR UNSIGHTLY SURROUND, LIGHTLY SANDED SALVAGED OAK BLOCKS ARE A SIMPLE BUT STURDY OPTION. A FIREPLACE REALLY DOES SET THE TONE FOR THE ROOM, SO CHOOSE CAREFULLY.

sofa that was built to last but has an ugly cover, don't take it at face value. Have it reupholstered, ideally in a neutral fabric to provide a calming backdrop to the rest of the room. Coarse natural linen makes a hardwearing cover. Leave the edges raw, use exaggerated stitches, patch where necessary and have the seams on show: make it look as though the cover is on inside out. This honesty fits in with the recycled philosophy. It doesn't matter if your seating looks a bit scruffy, especially in the case of old leather sofas and club chairs, as they improve with age and a bit of wear and tear. Old American metal glider chairs, designed for sipping lemonade on the porch, are an alternative and provide a total contrast in texture. Soften them with

a couple of cushions. A daybed with a curly iron frame can be converted into a more substantial couch by adding old wooden boards and a ticking mattress, blankets, and a collection of cushions made from recycled textiles. The mixture of opposing materials and styles works surprisingly well.

If you opt for a new sofa, go for the biggest you can afford or fit in your space. Choose any shape you like, bearing in mind that the ideal sofa for the recycled home is the simplest; curly edges, frills and flounces don't really dovetail with textured walls and wooden floors. The important thing is that there is room for everyone and that it's comfortable. Again, opt for neutral linen upholstery. If you want to pep it up with a bit of colour, cover cushions in vibrant

left Sticking to a blue, black and white colour palette makes a vivid graphic statement and allows more unusual recycled creations to really stand out, such as the hanging sculpture made from driftwood and other found objects, as well as the superb lacquered trunk that acts as a coffee table.

opposite A pile of cushions of various shapes and sizes adds colour to the neutral sofa. These tones are reflected in the intricate artwork behind, composed of scraps of handmade paper.

TAKE A WONKY OLD TABLE AND CUT ITS LEGS DOWN, OR USE A TIN TRUNK STRIPPED OF COLOUR TO REVEAL A SCRATCHY, SLIGHTLY SHINY METALLIC SURFACE – JUST THE RIGHT HEIGHT FOR A COFFEE TABLE.

patterned fabrics – if you tire of the pattern or colour at a later date, they are easier and cheaper to change than your sofa.

If funds and space allow, have two or even three sofas grouped together in comfortable chatting distance. If your room has a fireplace, let it dictate how you arrange your furniture; imagine where you'd like to sit on a winter evening. If you have a fireplace with a missing or unsightly surround, lightly sanded salvaged oak blocks are a simple but sturdy option. For something more traditional, cast-iron or wooden surrounds can be tracked down in salvage yards. A fireplace really does set the tone for the room, so choose carefully.

Once you have arranged your sofas, you will probably see the need for a low table on which to set cups of tea. We're not talking about a polished nest of tables, but a simpler recycled alternative. Consider taking a wonky old table and cutting its legs down, or using a tin trunk stripped of colour to reveal a scratchy, slightly shiny metallic surface – they are just the right height for a coffee table and will double as storage, too. A few small side tables at different heights are always handy. Curly wirework garden tables contrast well with a chunky sofa, or use an old bar stool with its seat spun down to the lowest level. Wide flat woven baskets picked up on travels abroad are a good option for stashing magazines. Don't just stick to one item, combine several for the true recycled look.

this page This sofa is a recycled version of modern modular sofa units. It was constructed using wooden planks and the ends of an old iron hospital bed. The mixture of styles in this room sit well together, unified by their neutral colour schemes.

opposite above More 'modular' seating made from rescued materials is perfectly countered by a chair that looks like a work of art in itself. It has sadly lost its upholstery, leaving behind a metal frame and ornate base, and has been subtly elevated on metal stilts. A couple of cushions make it a great spot for a sleeping cat.

opposite below Attention to detail is all-important here. The wood used to construct this bench seat is also used for the skirting boards, so the clean lines of the sofa are continued, adding to the light, airy feeling of the room.

right Patchwork ticking and stitched linen perk up this classically proportioned chair. The shelves, made from steel plate, add another contemporary edge.

below The loose cover on this chair is held in place by heavy thread looped through large metal eyelets. The nautical feel is completed with a driftwood shelf.

opposite A battered club chair looks perfect in this masculine living room, along with the rusty glider bench. A leather medicine ball and motorcycle helmet with goggles are ideal company for the huge model aeroplane, which makes an unusual focal point.

Storage is an important consideration in the living area, as so many different activities take place here. You need somewhere to shelve books and house your music collection. Multi-functional wooden fruit crates come in to their own in this room; hang as many as you need along a wall to create a bank of shelving. Pile up old metal tins or deed boxes with the paint stripped off, or create a mobile library of books in a rescued factory trolley.

With all the hustle and bustle of life neatly stored away, you can concentrate on displaying the things you love. The living room is the perfect place for this. Group together similarly hued items on white-painted shelves, or devote a tabletop to an arrangement of found objects. You can always stack books or old vinyl records underneath. Hang clusters of pictures on neutral walls, and don't choose art because it matches your furniture but find something original that you really like. Affordable works of art can be found at end-of-year shows at art colleges or at small independent galleries. For a more unusual display, string together a collection of beach finds and hang them in the living room to create your own piece of sculpture.

Lighting in the living room should be adaptable to all the activities that it hosts. Lots of individual lights work better than one single central light, and create an ideally relaxing atmosphere. You will probably need more sockets to accommodate them than you think. Mix and match lamp styles. Industrial articulated ones provide all-important contrast to the softness of the room, and look great partnered with a traditional standard lamp (which could be given a recycled home makeover). Floor lamps make useful reading lights; metallic 1960s-style ones that gracefully arc over a chair are good. Experiment with filament, clear and silvered lamp bulbs to create different moods (avoid the pearly ones). Candles and firelight make for cosy winter evenings.

bathrooms

The bathroom is where the notion of contrasts really comes into its own; it is an ideal place to experiment with different textures, surfaces and materials. The addition of some carefully chosen recycled items, large or small, creates a place that doesn't conform to the usual expectations of what a bathroom should be, softens its feeling of functionality and inspires individuality in the one room in the house where you really can get away from it all.

this page A pair of riding boots is given a humorous new role as toilet roll holders. The pristine bathroom fittings are countered by the soft chalkiness of the walls, which have been scraped clean (but not perfectly) of their paint. An unusual shelf houses toiletries.

opposite above left Wall-mounted bib taps support a convenient mirror.

opposite below left Stone balustrading holds a piece of old marble to form a sink stand. The splashback tiles came from a floor, the subtle stripe along the edges showing where they were lifted.

The bathroom should feel like a calm, clean relaxing haven, so don't allow it to take too much of a back seat in your decorating scheme. Rethink your approach to the bathroom. Why tile it from top to bottom? To give the room more definition, go for textured walls. If you want to seal the peeled-back paint, use a weak solution of flexible sealant; this waterproofs the walls, but you will lose the chalky finish. Not all the walls need to be stripped, however; treating just one works well with more finished areas. Another option is wooden panelling;

above A modern sink rests on an old bakery table, topped with weathered wooden planks. A stealthy battleship sits on the top of the mirror, which was, surprisingly, once covered in elaborate plaster relief.

old tongue-and-groove boards are particularly useful in the bathroom, but again panel a single wall to prevent it from being too overwhelming. Beautifully weathered wood gives the room a feeling of warmth and is extremely practical as it allows the room to breathe. Contrast textured walls with floorboards painted with flat white paint. This also gives a sensation of extra space, as white reflects light, and wood also feels friendly underfoot.

Once the walls and floors are established, it's time to consider the functional details. Look out for an old rolltop bath with clawed feet, or opt for a reproduction. However, be wary of old taps – it's likely they will have reached the end of their useful lives and need reseating or new washers. New, retro-style taps are widely available, but don't feel obliged

opposite The small details in this bathroom give it an air of the unexpected. Cartoonish modern taps contrast with a claw-footed rolltop bath. Toilet paper sits on a conveniently positioned hat stand, while the loo brush lives in an old flowerpot. Chipped dental shelves provide a home for bowls of soap.

this page A bath rack made from an old wooden herring tray slotted onto a piece of sawn ladder is an example of creative recycling.

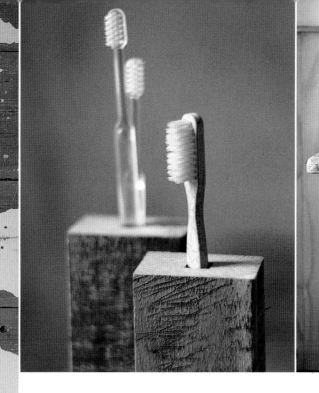

IF YOUR OLD BATH HAS A BROKEN LEG OR TWO, IT WILL LOOK JUST AS GOOD MOUNTED ON WEATHERED WOODEN BLOCKS.

above left Small oak blocks can be drilled to make unusual toothbrush holders.

above right A workbench has been transformed into a washstand, upon which sit a conical basin and modern tap.

opposite Flaky wooden boards fitted horizontally (rather than vertically, sauna style) give this bathroom a marine air. The floor was sanded smooth and painted white as a counterbalance. An old bath, which was rescued despite its missing legs, rests on sturdy wooden sleepers.

to match your taps to your old bath. Instead, have a bit of fun adding sleek modern taps, which can look amazing with a more traditional-style tub.

If you decide on an old bath and come across one with a broken leg or two, don't dismiss it out of hand. It will look just as good mounted on weathered wooden blocks. If the enamel of an old bath is a little chipped, simple repairs can be made using enamel from model-making shops. Rust can be removed using proprietary liquids and gels. If the surface of the bath is very worn, it is probably best left alone as re-enamelling is rarely done these days. Should your hunt prove fruitless, there are lots of brand new but traditional-looking bathtubs to choose from. If your bathroom is on the small side, a bath that fits along the wall can be given a recycled makeover by panelling it with wooden boards.

this page This neat bathroom cabinet, with inset sink, was made from wooden planks. The cabinet appears to be floating, which gives a feeling of extra space. The mismatched handles are an unexpected element, sure to make you take a second look.

opposite The same wooden planks were used slightly differently in this sister bathroom. The floor is made from slate mosaic tile and the walls are left unpainted.

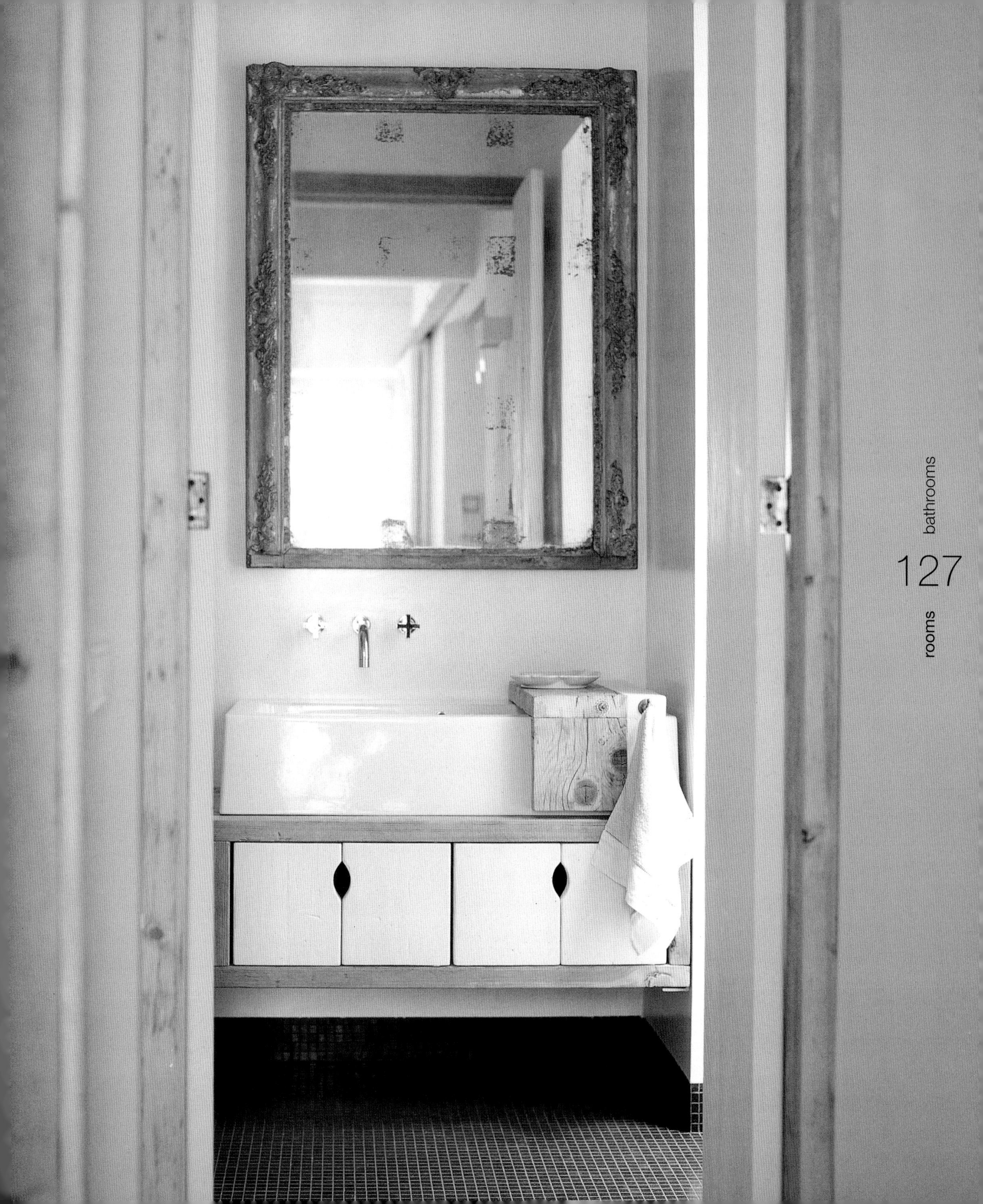

opposite This completely recycled outdoor wet room, built into the corner of an open-fronted barn, was made from a mix of rescued materials such as floorboards and reclaimed wooden panelling. It makes a perfect bathroom for hosing down muddy kids and pets.

right The interior is brightened up with casually hung, assorted mirrors with varying degrees of flaked silvering. An old linen sack acts as a bathmat. The sink is an original from the 1940s.

Basins give you plenty of opportunity to unleash your recycling creativity. A beautiful contemporary tap and basin look even better mixed with something unexpected, such as an old bakery table with a scaffold-board top. Alternatively, chunky Belfast sinks seem to be sneaking into the bathroom more and more. They look good resting on a stand made from thick wooden planks, which suit their robust personality. For smaller bathrooms, a sink on chrome-plated legs gives a feeling of space and extra room for hanging damp towels.

Your bathroom needs to feel warm. Old radiators are best bought direct from the house they are leaving: radiators from reclamation yards may have been left out for months in cold weather, and if they have frozen they crack, which is virtually impossible to fix. If in doubt, choose new ones. There are great alternatives in cast iron and steel. It's worth checking with a plumber what heat output is required for each room.

Mirrors are a good way to introduce the recycled look into your bathroom, and they increase light. Ornate gilt picture frames used as mirrors make a great contrast with the room's functionality. Go for mismatched styles, and it's definitely a case of the more the merrier. To keep your bathroom clutter-free, a wooden ladder makes a good drying rack for towels, or try cutting a section of broken ladder slightly longer than the width of your bath and topping it with a wooden seed tray to make a bath rack. Industrial work-in-progress trolleys make good storage for lotions and potions, as do medicine cabinets.

bedrooms

Bedrooms are all about serene simplicity and, of course, sleeping. Make it your aim to create an environment that is conducive to a good night's rest, the importance of which should never be underestimated. All your bedroom needs is a few simple recycled finds and a spark or two of imagination to create a cosy nest where you'll be sure to want to lie in on a Sunday morning … even if you do have the rest of the house to undecorate!

left This simple bed is made from solid oak blocks, while the headboard, screwed into the wall, is actually a piece of driftwood, formerly part of a ship's deck. Upturned dolly tubs are the perfect height for bedside tables and add contrasting texture too. Articulated French lamps cast a warm glow for bedtime reading.

below Scaffolding planks lend a recycled feel to a traditional headboard shape. Another surprise is the block-shaped bedside shelf, integral to the design.

opposite A balanced blend of natural woodiness and industrial lighting. Old inspection lamps sit on oak blocks, with their trailing wires making a graphic statement.

When you're rushed off your feet every day, your home should be as relaxed and restful as possible – and this applies tenfold to your bedroom. The textures and chalky tones of recycled home undecoration naturally promote a mellow ambience and so are perfect for this room, where you need to feel totally at ease. The textures of weathered wood, with its imperfections and signs of age, also seem peaceful. There's a certain something in recycled finds that modern furniture, with its shiny surfaces and smooth textures, lacks.

Of course the most important piece of furniture in your bedroom is the bed. Spending money on the most comfortable mattress for your sleeping style should be a priority, and this is one of the rare occasions when recycling isn't the answer – save that for the bed frame instead. There are many ways you can improvise here. If you come across a pair of old, slightly worn and paint-chipped iron bed ends, restore them from

their life in limbo. They can easily be fastened to a newer bed to give it a more lived-in look. A simple but sturdy alternative, which has a certain minimalist sensibility, is to create a frame out of wooden planks and rest it on large sawn green-oak planks. There is an honesty to a bed made this way, so whatever you do don't hide it away under a frilly valance. Another wooden option is a patchwork bed – and that's the actual frame, not the quilt. Use recycled wooden planks of subtly different hues to create a simple four-poster, a modern update of a tired classic. If you're after simple, unfussy lines, a structure made from scaffolding poles could be an industrial-style solution.

Dress your bed in clean earthy tones. Look out for old French linen. If you can't track down a perfect piece, buy a few oddments, cut them

opposite Make a feature out of construction details, more often than not hidden away. The joists of the oak-board bed become an interesting feature that suits the integrity of the materials.

opposite inset The rawness of the Shaker-style bed is well matched by this slouchy armchair covered in roughly painted canvas: an unexpected mix of modern art and functional furniture.

this page A recycled take on a four-poster gives an old-fashioned classic a fresh new look. An old linen tablecloth draped across the boards makes an unfussy canopy.

this page This child's bed, with curlicues reminiscent of Hansel and Gretel's gingerbread house, is made entirely from reclaimed wood: a mismatched patchwork of floorboards and panelling. The look is extended to a miniature table and chair.

opposite above Give yourself sweet dreams with beautiful grown-up mobiles hanging from your ceiling, such as this aeroplane made from a scrap piece of chicken wire.

opposite below A gorgeous silk panel, formerly a canopy from a four-poster, makes a dazzling, super-sized headrest. The room's monastic simplicity gives it the chance to shine.

up and stitch the good bits together. Linen is a classic, soft but hardwearing backdrop for more colourful bedcoverings, which need not necessarily have started life as bed linen. Use an old embroidered shawl, a bright crocheted throw or a wonderfully warm Welsh woollen blanket. You could even match (but not too carefully) a patchwork wooden bed by sewing together vintage fabric offcuts and segments of old clothes that are no longer quite wearable. Lots of layers keep you cosy and provide easy-on-the-eye contrasting colours and textures. When you peel back the covers, fresh, white bed linen is the best finishing touch for a colourful ensemble.

You need a bedside table to hold your book, the alarm clock and an easy-to-reach light. Make it large enough to prevent night-time avalanches, and of a height to suit the bed frame you have created. For utter simplicity, use an oak block or wooden fruit crate, or create a patchwork chunky cube from wood, architrave and skirting-board offcuts.

Adjustable lighting is indispensable in the bedroom. A twist of the dimmer switch is all you need to transport yourself from day to night. Bedside lamps don't have to be too pretty, it's the light they provide that creates the warm glow. So consider an old French inspection lamp with its

LINEN IS A CLASSIC, SOFT BUT HARDWEARING BACKDROP FOR MORE COLOURFUL BEDCOVERINGS SUCH AS AN OLD EMBROIDERED SHAWL OR A BRIGHT CROCHETED THROW.

metal cage, which is easy to fix wherever you need it most, or soften its look slightly by mounting one on a worn wooden block. A trusty filament bulb on extra-long corded flex can be hung from a nail tapped into the wall, or a hook screwed into the ceiling, for more movable lighting.

In an ideal world your bedroom wouldn't contain much more than your bed and a small table, but this demands extra storage space elsewhere. If you do have a small boxroom, consider vamping it up to create the luxury of a dressing room. A few

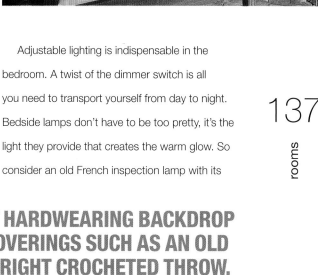

this page Touches of black give this bedroom a graphic edge. Old white fabric has been brought to life with an intricate pattern, screen-printed by the artistic owner of the house. The industrial-style bedside lamps, mounted on stands, balance the softer textures of the room. Disguising an ugly modern radiator with a piece of thin linen is a clever trick.

this page A piece of rescued wooden panelling has been turned on its side and employed as a sturdy headboard, providing a geometric backdrop to the clean lines of the bed and exposed wall timbers. An unusual lamp, made from dyed wool wrapped around a wire frame, rests on the patchwork wooden table. The unexpected touch of this lamp softens the whole bedroom, saving it from too much monastic austerity.

left This stunning bed, made from beautifully textured wood which once had a more mundane career as flooring, creates a self-contained world of sleep. Add a couple of cushions and it also doubles as a cosy daytime seating area.

right These well-placed rescued wooden planks prove just how simple and efficient recycled design can be. Resting gently against the wall, they function perfectly as an ergonomic headboard, holding you in just the right position for a quick read before lights out.

CREATE A FRAME OUT OF PLANKS AND REST IT ON LARGE SAWN GREEN-OAK PLANKS. THERE IS AN HONESTY TO A BED MADE THIS WAY, SO DON'T HIDE IT. ANOTHER OPTION IS A PATCHWORK BED – THAT'S THE FRAME, NOT THE QUILT.

scaffolding poles or lengths of galvanized piping (from a friendly plumbers' merchant) stretched from one end of the room to the other make simple hanging space for your clothes, and the whole construction is a much more satisfying use of spare-room space than merely piling it up with boxes and closing the door.

If you do keep your clothes in your bedroom, you need ample storage in order to keep the room as clutter-free as possible, so you don't feel crowded by your garments. Pick a few of your favourites to keep on display and hang the rest in a rescued wardrobe, or find old garment rails to turn into a wardrobe on wheels; this will allow you to check your wardrobe easily and weed out the things you haven't worn for a while. To complement the clothes that are going to be on display, look out for old wooden coat hangers, which often have faded shop names printed on them. They turn up at flea markets and car boot sales and are an inexpensive way of introducing recycled style into your home. If your crop of rescued hangers isn't large enough, use new ones and wrap them in leftover scraps of vintage fabric. If the sight of your expanding collection keeps you awake at night hide it behind a screen, which could be assembled from abandoned doors or shutters hinged together.

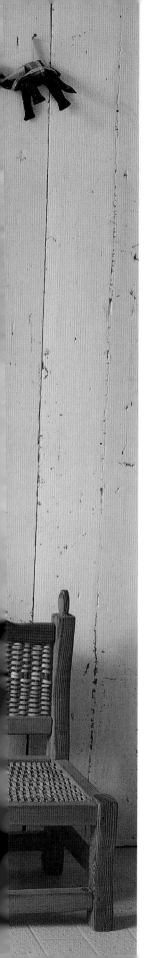

children's rooms

Children's rooms need to be functional and flexible, but are a good opportunity for a bit of fun as well. Introducing a few adaptable rescued creations allows you to nurture good taste, and encourages the habit of recycling at an early age. As the recycled look is not tied down by a struggle for perfection and making sure everything matches, it is ideal for the ever-changing needs of children's rooms, making it a cheaper option in the long run.

above Recycled wood makes beautiful furniture, perfect for the ever-changing needs of children's rooms. The scaffold boards used to create this classically good-looking cot could be transplanted to other projects in the home when the cot is no longer needed.

left An old easel blackboard, complete with tin for holding sticks of chalk, makes a perfect paper-saving spot for scrawling instant messages and lists or even creating miniature works of art.

WOODEN CRATES WORK WELL FOR STORAGE – EITHER STACKED AS TOY BOXES OR USED AS MODULAR-STYLE OPEN SHELVING, WHICH ALSO MEANS THAT FAVOURITE TOYS ARE HAPPILY ON DISPLAY.

Children's rooms should be a cosy little haven for your kids to escape into and let their imaginations run wild. Their rooms need to have the ability to change and adapt as they grow (and probably start to demand more and more possessions). Adopting the recycled look means that furniture additions, extensions and even the odd removal are easily achieved and the overall effect remains one of cohesion, but never bland uniformity.

Children's beds start off small and need to grow. If you create a simple initial structure, then all you really need is a new mattress and a few more wooden blocks and boards to complete an extension when required. Leave the wood unpainted and introduce colour with brightly patterned bed linen and colourful blankets, which can be changed or recycled somewhere else as favourite colours change.

above This child's room has been entirely furnished with rescued wooden creations. The scaffold-board doll's house has a new life as a quirky bookshelf. Beautiful wooden boxes make stackable storage, which can grow with the child's toy collection. The simple rug is stitched-together floor cloths, while the desk makes the most of the natural light streaming through the window.

left Rescued school chairs can be hung out of the way, waiting for the next visit from friends. Suspended like this, they take on a surreal, almost sculptural air.

below Well-crafted traditional toys make appealing playthings, even in today's high-tech world.

right Make a child's room a place of discovery and creativity. Blackboards make easy-to-clean cupboard doors, while wooden crates on wheels are perfect transport for toys. Keep an eye on the details. Vintage toys positioned in unexpected places, such as high up on a beam, add a sense of fun.

Storage is, as in all rooms, important, and again should be able to expand on demand. Wooden crates work well – either stacked as toy boxes or used as modular-style open shelving, which also means that favourite toys are happily on display. Old suitcases are another good way of stashing away treasures. Label them with brown luggage tags and they could encourage a keen sense of adventure.

Any furniture, and especially cupboards and chests of drawers, can be enlivened with a lick of blackboard paint or the occasional slightly wider blackboard plank. In this case drawing on the furniture won't be frowned upon, just make sure the creative urge stays where it is supposed to!

Well-crafted traditional toys made from natural rather than synthetic materials are long-lasting classics and will only improve with age. Making soft toys is a good way of using up scraps of vintage fabric or outgrown clothes, and again they will age

well as they become worn and slightly faded, in keeping with the recycled look. If these toys require a bit of mending and patching, it will suit them just fine. Encourage sweet dreams by hanging mobiles made of quirky recycled items or small toy cars or aeroplanes. Let your imagination run wild too.

work rooms

Working at home is on the increase as communication gets faster and easier, even for the most technophobic. Creating an office space in the recycled home gives you the opportunity to escape the beige blandness of the average workplace. You'll be glad to get up in the morning, and may even find yourself leaping out of bed and arriving at the office early – via the stairs or along the hallway, freshly brewed coffee in hand.

left A huge table makes an amazing communal desk, well positioned by a window to make the most of the light. The lamp, rescued from a jeweller's, is perfect for detailed work.

right This unusual collection of recycled finds makes for an inspirational office space. The contrast between the primitive wooden table and the sculptural 1950s chair is striking. The enormous pencil made from rolled-up card was part of a 1960s stationery shop display.

MAKE A DESK OUT OF A MISMATCHED TOP AND WHATEVER LEGS YOU CAN FIND OR RESCUE, SUCH AS A PAIR OF BUILDER'S TRESTLES TOPPED WITH AN OLD WOODEN DOOR.

The study or quiet corner where you work should be as beautiful as the rest of your home, not a replica of the dull office you've dreamt of escaping. Plan it carefully, and include the elements that keep any office running smoothly – filing especially. Bring an old metal filing cabinet back to life; giving an object its original function back is a considered bit of recycling. Separated from strip lighting and carpet tiles, these cabinets feel different, and shake off dull functionality. All sorts of recycled finds can keep your office in order. Large wooden trays with useful handles, rescued from ceramic factories, are excellent for storing papers and become even more efficient with wheels. Wicker fishing baskets are perfect for filing paperwork that you don't need instant access to. Old wooden tool boxes are also handy for office storage, as are smaller index drawers rescued from libraries.

Make your desk as big as you can. Don't worry about going too big, as you'll always be able to use the space. Position it by a window so you get the benefit of sunlight while you work (just don't get too distracted by the view). A 1950s-style metal desk is a good recycled find; rescue them from abandonment, as they're sadly no longer compatible with today's more manoeuvrable office furniture. Find a vintage French postal cabinet and your desk and storage problems are solved in one go. A spacious wooden desk always feels good to work on, as it has a warmth that you don't get from a glass or metal desktop. Make a desk out of a mismatched top and any legs you can find, such as a pair of builder's trestles topped off with an old wooden door. Make sure the

this page The modern computer is well contrasted by the plank desk and mismatched chairs (one originally from a dentist's surgery). The feeling of space here is ideal for some clear-headed thinking.

opposite above An old garden table with spindly metal legs is balanced by a sturdy industrial machinist's chair, made more comfortable for long hours at the desk with a squashy cushion.

opposite below A 1950s desk, stripped to reveal a scratched metal surface, goes perfectly with the textured wall. Vintage finds, such as a wire in-tray and a fan, make perfect accompaniments.

FORGET UGLY PLASTIC PUMP-ACTION CHAIRS ON WHEELS AND CONSIDER AN OLD FACTORY MACHINIST'S CHAIR. IF THE SEAT HAS SEEN BETTER DAYS, REPLACE IT: THE INDUSTRIAL METAL BASE WILL LAST A LIFETIME. WHATEVER YOU CHOOSE, ADD A CUSHION COVERED IN RESCUED FABRIC.

surface is smooth enough to work on comfortably. To keep your desk tidy, stash pens in old French confit jars or bread tins, and other stationery in old wooden seed trays and rescued wire in-trays.

Sit yourself down on a comfortable chair that supports your back and is the right height for your work, but forget ugly plastic pump-action chairs on wheels and consider an old factory machinist's chair instead. If the seat has seen better days, replace it: the industrial metal base will last a lifetime. Whatever you choose, add a cushion covered in rescued fabric.

Lighting is important in your office, especially if you spend long hours at your desk. If your desk is in a difficult corner, you need adaptable articulated lighting that is tall enough to illuminate your work. Try old anglepoise lamps, but in this case, new lighting designed for the job could be a better option.

Make your office space a motivating place to be by surrounding yourself with things that inspire you (rather than a dusty Swiss cheese plant). Fill a noticeboard with postcards, photos, fabric swatches or pages from magazines, or hang them, with small bulldog clips, from a length of string along one wall.

sources in the UK

furniture and accessories

Baileys

Whitecross Farm
Bridstow
Ross-on-Wye
Herefordshire HR9 6JU
01989 563015
www.baileyshome.com
*Our store – an amazing mix
of everything recycled (we
are biased).*

Caravan

www.caravanstyle.com
*Always fascinating. A place
to look at flea-market style.*

The Conran Shop

Michelin House
81 Fulham Road
London SW3 6RD
020 7589 7401
www.conranshop.co.uk
*Contemporary furniture
with some ethnic and
antique items.*

Liberty

Regent Street
London W1B 5AH
020 7734 1234
www.liberty.co.uk
*Stylish modern furniture,
tableware and accessories.*

Mint

www.mintshop.co.uk
*Stylish modern furniture,
ceramics and accessories.*

Paul Reeves

32B Kensington Church
Street
London W8 4HA
020 7937 1594
www.paulreeveslondon.com
*Arts and Crafts furniture
and lighting.*

Petersham Nurseries

Off Petersham Road
Richmond
Surrey TW10 7AG
020 8940 5230
www.petershamnurseries.com
*Great plants and antique
garden furniture.*

Robert Young Antiques

68 Battersea Bridge Road
London SW11 3AG
020 7228 7847
www.robertyoungantiques.com
*Folk art, furniture and
accessories.*

Selfridges

400 Oxford Street
London W1A 1AB
0800 123 400
www.selfridges.com
*Classic and cutting-edge
design for the home.*

Spencer Swaffer Antiques

30 High Street
Arundel
West Sussex BN18 9AB
01903 882132
www.spencerswaffer.com
Decorative antiques.

Squint

178 Shoreditch High Street
London E1 6HU
020 7739 9275
www.squintlimited.com
Sofas, armchairs and lamps.

Summerill and Bishop

100 Portland Road
London W11 4LN
020 7221 4566
www.summerillandbishop.com
French and Italian cookware.

antique and flea markets

There are many regular
antique fairs around the
country. Check these
websites for information:

www.antiques-atlas.com

www.gbaw.co.uk

markets in London

Portobello

Portobello Road, W11
*Friday and Saturday,
8am to 5pm.*
www.portobelloroad.co.uk

Brick Lane

Brick Lane, Cheshire Street,
Sclater Street, E1 and E2
Sunday, 6am to 1pm.

Bermondsey market

Bermondsey Square, SE1
Friday, 5am to 1pm.

Camden market

Camden High Street, NW1
Every day.
www.camdenlock.net

Greenwich market

Greenwich Church Street,
Stockwell Street, Greenwich
High Road, SE10
*Saturday and Sunday,
9.30am to 5pm.*
www.greenwich-market.co.uk

architectural salvage

The following carry a wide
selection of architectural
antiques, from doors and
panelling to smaller items.

Andy Thornton

Victoria Mills
Stainland Road
Greetland, Halifax
West Yorkshire HX4 8AD
01422 376000
www.andythornton.com

Minchinhampton Architectural Salvage

Cirencester Road
Aston Down
Stroud
Gloucestershire GL6 8PE
01285 760886
www.mascosalvage.com
*Decorative architectural
antiques.*

Salvo

www.salvo.co.uk
*Huge resource of salvage
yards and recycled materials.*

paint

Auro Organic Paints

01452 772020
www.auro.co.uk
*Natural emulsions, eggshells
and chalk paints in muted
colours. Also floor finishes
and wood stains.*

Earth Born

01928 734171
www.earthbornpaints.co.uk
*Environmentally friendly
paints.*

Nutshell Natural Paints

01392 823760
www.nutshellpaints.co.uk
*Natural paints, Swedish floor
soap and waxes for wood.*

sources in the US

furniture and accessories

ABC Carpet & Home

888 Broadway
New York, NY 10003
212 473 3000
Visit the website for a retail
outlet near you.

www.abchome.com
*An eclectic collection of
furnishings, linens, rugs and
other home accessories.*

Altered Antiques

www.altered-antiques.com
*New ways to use old things,
such as furniture crafted from
salvaged wood and metal.*

Anthropologie

www.anthropologie.com
*One-of-a-kind home
accessories, including
decorative hooks, boxes,
cupboard knobs and racks.*

The Conran Shop

Bridgemarket
407 East 59th Street
New York, NY 10022
866 755 9079

www.conranusa.com
*Modern furniture for every
room, plus storage items.*

Knoll

Phone 800 343 5665 or visit
the website for showrooms.
www.knoll.com
Modern and ergonomic lamps.

Moenia Design

2325 Third Street, Suite 226
San Francisco, CA 94107
253 395 3131

www.moeniadesign.com
*A wide selection of baskets
offers both storage and style.*

Ochre

462 Broome Street
New York, NY 10013
212 414 4332

www.ochre.net
*Contemporary furniture,
antiques, accessories
and lighting.*

Pottery Barn

1965 Broadway
New York, NY 10023
212 579 8477

www.potterybarn.com
*Contemporary furniture and
accessories for the home.*

R 20th Century Design

82 Franklin Street
New York, NY 10013
212 343 7979

www.r20thcentury.com
*Includes a comprehensive
selection of mid-century
lamps and lighting fixtures.*

Restoration Hardware

935 Broadway
New York, NY 10010
212 260 9479
Visit the website for an
outlet near you.

www.restorationhardware.com
*Fine hardware, including
lighting, also furniture and
accessories for the home.*

flea markets

The Annex Antique Fair and Flea Market

West 39th Street and Ninth
Avenue, New York
212 243 5343

www.hellskitchenfleamarket.com
*Manhattan's primary flea
market takes place every
Saturday and Sunday.*

Brimfield Antique Show

Route 20
Brimfield, MA 01010
www.brimfieldshow.com
*This famous flea market,
which features dealers from
all over the U.S. and from
Europe, runs for a week in
May, July and September.*

Englishtown Auction Sales

90 Wilson Avenue
Englishtown, NJ 07726
732 446 9644

www.englishtownauction.com
*This 100-acre market attracts
professional and amateur
dealers. Open Saturday
and Sunday, year-round.*

Rose Bowl Flea Market

100 Rose Bowl Drive
Pasadena, CA
323 560 7469

www.rgcshows.com
*On the second Sunday of
every month, everything from
retro kitsch to fine furnishings.*

architectural salvage, restoration, and antiques

Architectural Accents

2711 Piedmont Road NE
Atlanta, GA 30305
404 266 8700

www.architecturalaccents.com
*Antique light fixtures, door
hardware, garden antiques
and other reclaimed items.*

Architectural Paneling, Inc.

979 Third Avenue
New York, NY 10022
212 371 9632

www.apaneling.com
*Reproduction fireplaces and
architectural features.*

Caravati's Inc.

104 East Second Street
Richmond, VA 23224
804 232 4175

www.caravatis.com
*Restoration materials and
architectural details from
old buildings.*

Harrington Brass Works

201 818 1300

www.harringtonbrassworks.com
*Brass fixtures for kitchen and
home, especially taps/faucets.
Also bathroom products.*

Salvage One Architectural Elements

1840 W. Hubbard
Chicago, IL 60622
312 733 0098

www.salvageone.com
Architectural artifacts.

paint

Benjamin Moore Paints

101 Paragon Drive
Montvale, NJ 07645
Visit the website for
stockists.

www.benjaminmoore.com
Fine paints.

The Old Fashioned Milk Paint Company

436 Main Street
Groton, MA 01450
978 448 6336

www.milkpaint.com
*These paints, made from
natural pigments, replicate the
colour and finish of Colonial
and Shaker antiques.*

picture credits

Key: **a**=above, **b**=below, **r**=right, **l**=left, **c**=centre.

All photography by Debi Treloar, all images Mark and Sally Bailey's home in Herefordshire unless specified below.

Page 1 co-founder and creative director of Eleanor Home, Sune Jehrbo's home in Copenhagen; **4** private residence; **5** design: Cecilia Proserpio, furniture: Katrin Arens; **9ac & cl** Joel Bernstein's home in London; **9c** owner of Squint, Lisa Whatmough's London home; **9cr** Spazio Rossana Orlandi – exhibition of the Design Academy of Eindhoven during the Tabula Rasa event; **9bl** Mathilde Labrouche of Coté Pierre's home in Saintonge; **9br** Mark and Sally Bailey's former home in Herefordshire; **10al & cl** Liz Connell's home in London; **10ac & cr** Mathilde Labrouche of Coté Pierre's home in Saintonge; **10ar** Mark and Sally Bailey's former home in Herefordshire; **10c** design: Cecilia Proserpio, furniture: Katrin Arens; **10br** owner of Squint, Lisa Whatmough's London home; **15l** Roger Capps, home near Builth Wells; **15r** design: Cecilia Proserpio, furniture: Katrin Arens; **17 both** Mark and Sally Bailey's former home in Herefordshire; **19** Roger Capps, home near Builth Wells; **20** Mathilde Labrouche of Coté Pierre's home in Saintonge; **22** Roger Capps, home near Builth Wells; **23al & c** Spazio Rossana Orlandi; **23cl** Carole and Dominique de Laâge, artist, painter, and journalist, home in Charente-Maritime; **23cr** Martin Nannestad Jørgensen; **23bc** Mathilde Labrouche of Coté Pierre's home in Saintonge; **23br** Mark and Sally Bailey's former home in Herefordshire; **24l** Joel Bernstein's home in London; **24r** design: Cecilia Proserpio, furniture: Katrin Arens; **25r** Lucille and Richard Lewin's London house; **28** Joel Bernstein's home in London; **29** design: Cecilia Proserpio, furniture: Katrin Arens; **30–31** Mathilde Labrouche of Coté Pierre's home in Saintonge; **32 & 33r** Mark and Sally Bailey's former home in Herefordshire; **33l** private residence; **34a** Martin Nannestad Jørgensen; **34b** Joel Bernstein's home in London; **35** Mathilde Labrouche of Coté Pierre's home in Saintonge; **37l & r** Mark and Sally Bailey's former home in Herefordshire; **38–39** Katrin Arens; **40 & 41c** owner of Squint, Lisa Whatmough's London home; **41a all, cr, bc, & br** Mark and Sally Bailey's former home in Herefordshire; **42l** Martin Nannestad Jørgensen; **42ar & 43** Joel Bernstein's home in London; **44** private residence; **45c** co-founder and creative director of Eleanor Home, Sune Jehrbo's home in Copenhagen; **45r** Katrin Arens; **46** Mathilde Labrouche of Coté Pierre's home in Saintonge; **47 & 48al** Roger Capps, home near Builth Wells; **48b** Mark and Sally Bailey's former home in Herefordshire; **50** Roger Capps, home near Builth Wells; **51 & 52** Mathilde Labrouche of Coté Pierre's home in Saintonge; **53** Roger Capps, home near Builth Wells; **54** Spazio Rossana Orlandi; **57r** Mark and Sally Bailey's former home in Herefordshire; **60 & 61ar** Martin Nannestad Jørgensen; **61al** Joel Bernstein's home in London; **61br** Katrin Arens; **64, 65 main, & ar** owner of Squint, Lisa Whatmough's London home; **65bl** design: Cecilia Proserpio, furniture: Katrin Arens; **67l** Liz Connell's home in London; **70** Lucille and Richard Lewin's London house; **71ac & bl** Mark and Sally Bailey's former home in Herefordshire; **71ar** Joel Bernstein's home in London; **71cl** Martin Nannestad Jørgensen; **71c** owner of Squint, Lisa Whatmough's London home; **71bc** Liz Connell's home in London; **72 & 73r** Lucille and Richard Lewin's London house; **73l** Mathilde Labrouche of Coté Pierre's home in Saintonge; **76** Mark and Sally Bailey's former home in Herefordshire; **77l** Martin Nannestad Jørgensen; **77r** Mathilde Labrouche of Coté Pierre's home in Saintonge; **78l** Mark and Sally Bailey's former home in Herefordshire; **78r** owner of Squint, Lisa Whatmough's London home; **79** design: Cecilia Proserpio, furniture: Katrin Arens; **80 both** owner of Squint, Lisa Whatmough's London home; **81l** Mark and Sally Bailey's former home in Herefordshire; **81r** Joel Bernstein's home in London; **82** owner of Squint, Lisa Whatmough's London home; **83** Roger Capps, home near Builth Wells; **84 all & 85a** owner of Squint, Lisa Whatmough's London home; **85b** Joel Bernstein's home in London; **86–87** Martin Nannestad Jørgensen; **88 & 89l** Katrin Arens; **90 & 91a** Mathilde Labrouche of Coté Pierre's home in Saintonge; **91b** Roger Capps, home near Builth Wells; **94–95** Katrin Arens; **96–97** Martin Nannestad Jørgensen; **98–99** design: Cecilia Proserpio, furniture: Katrin Arens; **100–101** Spazio Rossana Orlandi; **102–103** Lucille and Richard Lewin's London house; **104 both** Joel Bernstein's home in London; **104–105** Katrin Arens; **107l** Lucille and Richard Lewin's London house; **108–9** Lucille and Richard Lewin's London house; **110–111** Mark and Sally Bailey's former home in Herefordshire; **112–113** Joel Bernstein's home in London; **114–115** design: Cecilia Proserpio, furniture: Katrin Arens; **116a** Joel Bernstein's home in London; **116b** co-founder and creative director of Eleanor Home, Sune Jehrbo's home in Copenhagen; **117** Mark and Sally Bailey's former home in Herefordshire; **118** Roger Capps, home near Builth Wells; **119l** Liz Connell's home in London; **121al** Joel Bernstein's home in London; **121bl** Mathilde Labrouche of Coté Pierre's home in Saintonge; **125 both** Mark and Sally Bailey's former home in Herefordshire; **126–127** design: Cecilia Proserpio, furniture: Katrin Arens; **128–129** Mathilde Labrouche of Coté Pierre's home in Saintonge; **130** Katrin Arens; **131** design: Cecilia Proserpio, furniture: Katrin Arens; **132b** design: Cecilia Proserpio, furniture: Katrin Arens; **133** Mark and Sally Bailey's former home in Herefordshire; **134** Katrin Arens; **135 both** Joel Bernstein's home in London; **136–137** Mathilde Labrouche of Coté Pierre's home in Saintonge; **138** Liz Connell's home in London; **139** Mathilde Labrouche of Coté Pierre's home in Saintonge; **140** Mathilde Labrouche of Coté Pierre's home in Saintonge; **141–145** Katrin Arens; **146b** Martin Nannestad Jørgensen; **148** Joel Bernstein's home in London; **149l** Mark and Sally Bailey's former home in Herefordshire; **149r** Liz Connell's home in London; **150** private residence; **152** design: Cecilia Proserpio, furniture: Katrin Arens; **153** Mark and Sally Bailey's former home in Herefordshire.

Endpapers: Illustrations by Charlotte Farmer.

designers whose work is featured in this book

Capps & Capps Limited

The Sawmill
Sarnesfield
Herefordshire HR4 8RH
+44 (0)1544 318877
fax +44 (0)1544 318399
www.cappsandcapps.com
Repair of old buildings.
Pages 15l, 19, 22, 47, 48al,
50, 53, 83, 91b, 118

Carole and Dominique de Laâge

La Braude
17130 St Maurice de
Laurençanne
France
+33 (0)6 70 06 30 34
Page 23cl

Cecilia Proserpio

cecilia.proserpio@fastwebnet.it
Pages 5, 10c, 15r, 24r, 29,
65bl, 79, 98–99, 114–115,
126–127, 131, 132b, 152

Coté Pierre

Chez Douteau Messac
17130 Montendre
France
+33 (0)5 46 86 47 44
mobile +33 (0)6 09 71 30 29
mathilde@cotepierre.com
www.cotepierre.com
Pages 9bl, 10ac, 10cr, 20,
23bc, 30–31, 35, 46, 51, 52,
73l, 77r, 90, 91a, 121bl,
136–137, 139, 140

Eleanor Home

info@eleanorhome.dk
www.eleanorhome.com
+45 7022 8085
fax +45 7022 8083
Pages 1, 45c, 116b

Katrin Arens

info@katrinarens.it
www.katrinarens.it
Pages 5, 10c, 15r, 24r,
29, 38–39, 45r, 61br,
65bl, 79, 88, 89l, 94–95,
98–99, 104–105, 114–115,
126–127, 130, 131, 132b,
134, 141–145, 152

Liz Connell

liz.connell@btopenworld.com
A selection of Liz's fabric
designs is available at
Borderline Fabrics:
+44 (0)20 7823 3567
www.borderlinefabrics.com
Pages 10al, 10cl, 67l, 71bc,
119l, 138, 149r

Lucille Lewin

Chiltern Street Studio
78a Chiltern Street
London W1U 5AB
+44 (0)20 7486 4800
fax +44 (0)20 7486 4840
www.chilternstreetstudio.com
Pages 25r, 70, 72, 73r,
102–103, 107l, 108–109

Martin Nannestad Jørgensen

www.martinnannestad.dk
Pages 23cr, 34a, 42l, 60,
61ar, 71cl, 77l, 86–87,
96–97, 146b

Spazio Rossana Orlandi

Via Matteo Bandello 14
20123 Milan
Italy
+39 (0)2 46 74 47 244
info@rossanaorlandi.com
www.rossanaorlandi.com
Pages 9cr, 23al, 23c, 54,
100–101

Squint Limited

178 Shoreditch High Street
London E1 6HU
www.squintlimited.com
Pages 9c, 10br, 40, 41c,
64, 65 main, 65ar, 71c, 78r,
80 both, 82, 84 all, 85a

picture credits

recycled home

index

Figures in *italics* indicate illustrations and captions.

acknowledgments

The making of *Recycled Home* started with a whirlwind of seventeen locations in seventeen days – involving much running for buses and flagging down of taxis, all while struggling under the weight of cases and bags of unwieldy photographic equipment! The people who kindly opened their doors to us not only let us disrupt their homes but also kept us fed and watered too, for which we are incredibly grateful. In particular, we would like to thank the following:

Mathilde Labrouche, interior and furniture designer using found objects and architectural elements (www.cotepierre.com).

Katrin Arens, furniture, interior and clothes designer working with abused wooden planks. She also makes kids' clothes stitched from grown-ups' hand-me-downs.

Rossana Orlandi, unofficial patron of the recycling movement. She has a gallery and cafe in an old tie factory in Milan.

Roger Capps of Capps and Capps historical building repair.

Lisa Whatmough, furniture designer at Squint and the queen of wrap.

Liz Connell, sculptor and printmaker.

Martin Nannestad Jørgensen, extraordinary weaver and occasional lecturer.

Sune Jehrbo, furniture and interior designer (www.eleanorhome.com).

Mark and Sally would like to thank all the people who let us into their inspiring recycled homes: Joel Bernstein, Lucille and Rick Lewin, Cecilia Proserpio, and Carole and Dominique de Laâge.

Thanks also to Alison and Paul, Emily, Clare (for being so patient with us), and everyone else at Ryland Peters and Small.

Thanks to Debi Treloar, a great photographer and lots of fun to work with, also her assistant Kiara who was particularly brilliant with her driving and translating on the Italian leg of our photography tour.

Thank you to Charlotte Farmer and her skills with a pen – both in her illustrations and help with the writing – and Gary for his woodworking skills.

Finally a big thanks to Ben and Lucy (our kids), Lorna Sproston, and everyone at Baileys who held it all together while we did this.

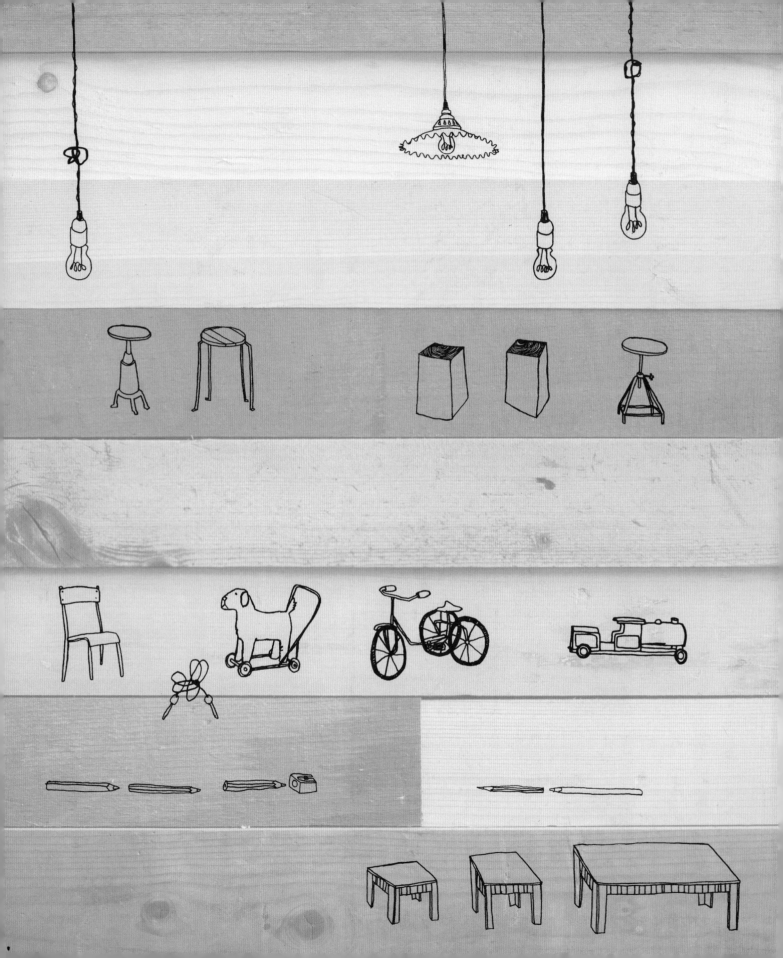